Money Mindset, Method & Mechanism

An Entrepreneur's Journey from Trapped on A Job to Freedom Working from Home

... and the Most Important Things I Ever Learned About Business and Money.

By Dexter Nelson

Money Mindset, Method & Mechanism
An Entrepreneur's Journey from Trapped on A Job to Freedom Working from Home

Contents

- Introduction
- Chapter 1 – Stuck Between Overload and A Catch-22   Page 7
- Chapter 2 – The Most Important Financial Skill   Page 19
- Chapter 3 – The Money Mindset   Page 21
- Chapter 4 – Money & Mindset Lessons   Page 43
- Chapter 5 – Bonus Lessons   Page 62
- Chapter 6 – Method & Mechanism   Page 68
- Chapter 7 – Resources and Recommended Learning   Page 77

Introduction

Welcome to the **Money Mindset, Method & Mechanism**, what I call the 4Ms of making money.

Unlike the typical business book this book isn't about teaching concepts and ideas, though you will find many; and while my hope is that you will be inspired, this is not an inspirational story book to hype you up either.

It's about my journey as an entrepreneur, and teaching the mindsets, methods, and mechanisms of how to make money from home as I've learned them.

What I share in this book are the most important lessons I've ever learned about business, and they were the most practical and applicable lessons that helped me to achieve my goals.

My hope is that they will be practical and applicable lessons for you to achieve your goals as well.

But before we get into all of that, it's important to me that you know who I am, and why I'm qualified to write this book.

My name is Dexter Nelson and as of June 3rd, 2020, I have been working full time from home for 8 years. I am the founder of two companies; a tech company, (TechDex Development & Solutions, founded in 2004), and a music company, (Echoingwalls Music, founded in 2000).

Over the course of the last 8 years, I've also become an avid student of sales, marketing, finance, and business, learning from mentors and other successful business owners.

I've always had the entrepreneurial bug and I've wanted to become a millionaire ever since childhood, but I wouldn't truly start my journey until years later after many setbacks, failures, and hardships.

Why it took me so long to move is one of the lessons that I learned, (and will share), and this book will be filled with my own hard-learned lessons, as well as real stories of my life, both personal and in business.

What I believe qualifies me to write this book, isn't just about what I do now, or even what I know, or who I've learned from, but also what I've done and had to overcome.

I started my entrepreneurial journey years ago, just after I got out of trade school, and for years it would be on and off efforts. I'd try an opportunity, make a little bit of money, realize it's not for me, then move on.

That's how it went for years, but there was never a pressing reason for me to put in the work and do this full time, then the economy crashed. If you remember the 2009 crash, then you remember how bad it was.

I went from making good money to being out of work for 18 months, which led to me being broke and basically relying on my family to get by.

Up until that point, the companies I started were just projects to supplement my income. I'd fix some PCs and build a website here or promote an album there; they were always good for a few hundred dollars extra per month.

I relied on that money, even as I burned through my savings, all while looking for steady work, but all I found were either part-time or seasonal work.

Eventually, that money dried up too, and I ended up where most people do when they reach their breaking point – broke, angry, and desperate to make money.

The worst part is that the people around me, my family, they were the ones who I took out all of my anger and frustration on. I wasn't a very good person back then.

I was at my "bottom" and after a few close calls with the cops, I knew I had to change.

I started reading self-improvement books and studying motivational material, and even started back on the entrepreneurial path because even though I had decided to change, it didn't mean my need to make money went away.

I didn't have a car anymore, so finding a job had to be something local, and for a while, I walked about 5 miles to work in the morning, and one of my coworkers would drop me home on evenings; plus, people would come and pick me up and drop me off from all of the side jobs I picked up.

My situation hadn't changed, so making money from home became more important than ever, and as I struggled through, I found someone who would become a mentor to me and a friend.

I had seen him at one of those hotel business meetings, and I had heard his story and was inspired by it because even though it was different, it was my story too.

We connected on Facebook and I decided to trust him when he presented me with an opportunity to make money from home. I jumped in, and I haven't looked back since.

That was June 3rd, 2012, and even though I've been home for all of these years trying to make money from home, and even though I've been in and out of opportunities before, that is the day that I consider the official first day of my entrepreneurial journey.

I consider it my first day because it was the day that I make my first deliberate steps to making money from home, and it reinforced what I already knew from before; I knew beyond any shadow of a doubt I had to be successful at making money from home because there was nothing else but poverty and misery for me if I didn't.

I leaned into it hard and committed myself like never before.

I was so green. I had a lot of growing to do, a lot of maturing to do, and there was a lot about business and money I had to learn.

And as I applied what I learned, I watched my income go from nothing, and gradually increase, to where I am now, finally able to provide for myself and help my family instead of being a burden.

And I'll be honest. I never thought it was that big of a deal. After all, I was just doing what I had to do as anyone would, right?

But then, people started asking me to teach them how to do what I did, especially after the pandemic lockdowns started, and one day, (I'm not sure what I was doing exactly), I stopped and had a realization that really changed how I see myself.

That realization was that I had done what I set out to do all those years ago.

True, I wasn't a millionaire, (I'm still not at the time of writing this), but the money was never really the point of me wanting to be one anyway.

All those years back when I was working regular jobs what I wanted was out. It wasn't the money I wanted; it was the lifestyle.

I was tired of waking up hours before the sun came up and commuting 2 hours one way to go to work and coming home late at night just exhausted.

I was tired of busting my butt moving furniture, and working on farms, and climbing ladders with bags of concrete on my back; going to work on some construction site in the middle of winter with three layers of clothes on and still feeling cold, tired, and sore all the time.

I wanted freedom and I wanted a lifestyle that allowed me to have that freedom and have some measure of control over, and to set my own schedule.

The money was always just a means to an end for me, and I realized at that moment that I had done it.

I had successfully learned how to make money from home, and not only did I successfully transition to doing it, but I had dug my way out of tremendous hardships to get there.

That's no small feat, and the best part is that I didn't have to become a millionaire to do it. All I had to do was replace the income I used to make, then make a little bit more so I didn't struggle.

Now, don't get me wrong.

The journey wasn't all smooth sailing. There were ups and downs, good times and bad, especially in the first few years where I wasn't quite making enough money to cover everything I needed to; and there still are bumps in the road and will always be.

That's just life.

But, with a lot of learning, patience, hard work, humility, and by the unending grace of God, I watched my income grow month after month, year after year, and now I'm here, as I said, able to provide for myself and to be able to help my family, all while working from home.

The personal development paid off too.

Men will know how this feels and I'm not sure I can explain it so women can understand, but our society is driven around men being providers, especially financially.

It's a part of my faith as a Christian and it's part of societal traditions and standards.

It's part of a man's identity and a part of our purpose on this planet, and as a man, when I couldn't do that, there was this deep-seated shame and a profound sense of worthlessness I felt.

And when people, including friends and family, would call me a loser or a failure, or ask, *"what kind of man are you?"* or tell me *"be a real man and get a job,"* or any of the dozen or so statements that connected my sense of manhood to the amount of money I made, it only deepened that shame because I knew they were right because I already felt that way about myself.

Now, I'm not arguing whether it's right or wrong that how much money a man makes should be associated with his manhood, or even if I was right or wrong for believing that a man should be able to provide for himself and his family, (and I do).

That's a whole different book entirely.

What I'm saying is, as I continued to grow and make more money, that shame lessened and eventually went away, and along with it, so did the anger.

The result is that I was no longer the same person I used to be.

I became a better person, reconnected with my faith and started living it, forged stronger and healthier relationships with friends and family, and I can honestly look at my life and feel something I don't think I've ever truly felt before – contentment.

I am proud of who I've become; of who God made me.

I'm writing this book because of who I am and what I've been able to accomplish.

I realize now that I've done something that very few people ever do, but many people wish to, but maybe they've never had the opportunity or the knowledge, and I feel that I have a duty to share what I know and what I've learned.

This book began as a personal exercise for me to recount and reinforce everything I've learned about money and business. It wasn't meant to be published for anyone but myself.

It seems selfish now not to share knowledge that can help someone else, and if even one person is helped by this book, then my time will not have been wasted.

Throughout this book, I'm going to share everything I've learned about business and money that I believe had a direct impact on my ability to make money from home.

All I ask in return is that you take the information seriously and that you do your best to implement what you're learning.

For perspective, currently, clients pay me around $3,000 to consult and help them implement plans to help them get results; some of them even more.

What you're going to learn here are things I don't share with paid clients, and in my opinion, is infinitely more valuable, so treat this as if you've paid me at least the same as any of my other clients.

That being said, let's get started.

The first thing I'm going to address before we get into the first M, (money mindset), I want to talk about a catch-22 and some of the problems I immediately faced when starting my journey.

Not too many people talk about this, but I feel it's important because I believe that this is the real reason why people quit before they even get started.

Chapter 1 – Stuck Between Overload and A Catch-22

Speaking from personal experience, if you want to make money from home, whether it's just a few hundred bucks extra per month, or replace your entire income so you can quit your job, or even create real and lasting wealth, you will quickly find that you are immediately met with a few problems; three in particular.

The first problem is the quantity of information.

If you were to search for the phrase *how to make money from home,* you will discover pretty quickly that there are quite literally **billions** of results.

When I searched, there were 4.5 billion results!

gle | how to make money from home

Q All   ▶ Videos   📰 News   🏷 Shopping   📖 Books

About 4,520,000,000 results (0.71 seconds)

That's crazy!

There is an endless trove of information and advice that you can consume, and every week there seems to be a new guru or expert that pops up with a new idea or scheme.

To be honest, it can be pretty overwhelming, and it often is.

I know it was overwhelming for me when I decided that I wanted to learn how to make money from home. I'm not even sure how to begin calculating the amount of time I spent searching for something that looked like it might work.

The second problem is the quality of information.

Again, speaking from experience, I think most of the information you'll find is pretty useless; at least it was to me. I'm not saying that the information wasn't good, although I did find information that was pure trash and did not work.

What I'm saying is that not all information is useful, or even relevant.

Some information was generalized, meaning that it's good, but it's not information I could have applied to get a result. Some of it was highly situational and could only be useful in certain, specific situations.

And then there was the information that was simply outdated and no longer effective.

That's the trickiest information of all because it used to work in the past, and it still seems like good, solid information, but for whatever reason, it just doesn't work anymore.

Markets evolve, trends change, technology gets better…

You'd be surprised how many people are wasting time and money trying to achieve results with outdated information. I know because I was one of them.

I've tried at least a dozen opportunities over the years and even as they were failing, I kept telling myself was that they should have worked.

Did I mention I was green and had a lot to learn?

Learning to identify what programs would work and what wouldn't work became one of those intuitive skills I developed, and one you will have started to do as well by the time you're done reading this book.

The third problem is the biggest one of all and the reason why I believe most people will *never* accomplish their goals because it's that big of a roadblock.

The problem is trust, or rather, the lack of it.

Let's say that you are willing to put in the time to search for an opportunity, and let's also say that you're willing to test drive those opportunities to see if they work.

How do you know what opportunity is legit, or even legal?

With all of the information out there, and new gurus and experts popping up all over the place, how do you know if the offer you're seeing is real or fake?

Or how do you know the person you're seeing is an actual expert that practices what they're preaching, or that the results that they're showing you are their actual results?

After all, experience matters, but so does integrity, am I right?

This is why I took the time to properly introduce myself and tell you all about me. I am an easily verifiable person.

Anyway, when I was first starting out, I ran into all of these problems and more, and I personally know people who started around the same time I did, that has since quit.

And if you're reading this book right now, I have to assume that you want to know how to make money from home. I'll also go out on a limb and say that you might have run into one of those problems too.

And if you haven't, count yourself fortunate to have avoided so much frustration, and wasted time and money.

So, when it comes to making money from home, where do you go? Who do you trust? What information is the right information for you?

Everyone knows you're supposed to invest time, money, or both into education, training, and whatever business or venture you start, but how can you invest anything into something you don't trust.

And something tells me the old *"give it time to work"* and attitude is not for you.

See, I've tried a lot of different things that didn't work and every time someone approached me about an opportunity, I needed to know that it was going to work because I didn't have time or money to waste on yet another *thing* that "had potential" and "could possibly" make good money.

That is typically what people who aren't making money in an opportunity tell people about the opportunity they're in and want the people they're talking to, to join.

Don't get me wrong, I'm not knocking hard-working people here. It takes courage to try something new and to dedicate time, money, and energy to build a business.

Not all business models work, and some only work for a short time, meaning they aren't sustainable.

But there are business models that do work, and to make them work you're going to have to do some things that you don't want to do in order to make money.

Have you ever looked at someone and thought, *"am I going to have to do what this person is doing to make this business work?"* and then decide you don't want to do what they're doing?

Don't feel bad if the answer is yes. I have too.

Here's a story about what happened to me early on when I learned that not all business opportunities are made equal.

I call it my catch-22 story.

I was fresh out of school with a brand-new certification in network engineering and was caught in a situation where nobody in my field was hiring newbies. Basically, they all wanted field experience to hire, but I couldn't get experience if nobody would hire me.

That was my catch-22.

Anyway, what ended up happening was me working a $9.00 per hour job for one of those rent-to-own furniture and appliance places, where my responsibility was being a driver, as well as the computer repair guy.

One day, this sharp-looking gentleman, older, saw me fixing the computers. He watched me for a while like he was interested, but I didn't pay him any mind. He wasn't the first person to be curious and thought it was cool how I could fix computers.

After I got one of the computers up and running, he approached me and said, "*you're a pretty bright young man*".

"*Thanks,*" I replied. "*I appreciate that. How can I help you?*" I asked, assuming he was another curious customer.

He smiled, reached out, shook my hand, introduced himself, and we started talking. He was curious about how I like my job and what my goals were, and he told me about himself and what he does, and then he asked me something that hooked me.

He asked, "*what on Earth is someone like you doing working in a place like this, and not some big tech giant out there? You certainly have the skills. How did you end up here?*"

And just like that, with one question, he cut right to the heart of all of the frustrations I've had since getting my certifications, so I told him my story and the catch-22 I was in.

He empathized and said, "*while I can't do anything about getting you a job in a big tech company, there is something I can do that might help you at least make some more money*".

At this point, I was really curious, because even back then $9.00 per hour wasn't much money after taxes, so I said, "*Okay. I'm listening*".

"*I'm in need of a few bright, tech-savvy people and I think we can help each other, and I'll tell you more, but not now,*" he said.

"*You're at work and I don't want to get you in trouble*".

He invited me to lunch the next day, on him, handed me his card as he shook my hand again, said "*I'll talk with you soon. It was nice meeting you,*" and left.

I was so excited! The whole day I was wondering what he needed people like me for, and just how much more money could I make?

I mean, if I could make as money as I would have at a big tech company, would my catch-22 even matter anymore?

I love the tech field and I love what I do, but I had to be real with myself too. Confronted with the possibility of making more money than I was making at the time, and possibly making more money than I would have, had I gotten any of the jobs in the field I trained for…

I'd take the money and skip the job.

So, the next day, dressed in my best pair of sneakers, khakis, and a polo shirt, I walked into a Shiny Dinner restaurant and was met by my new friend, and we sat down together.

We ordered lunch, talked for a while, and after lunch and the table was cleared, he said, "*I have something I want to show you*".

He then pulled out this big black binder and put it on the table. He looked at me dead in the eyes, pointed down at the folder, and said, "*This is why I need tech-savvy people like you*".

"*Finally!*" I thought but didn't say it. I just smiled and nodded my head repeatedly.

And for the next 15 minutes, I listened to this man talk about tiers, and pay plans, and shopping portals, and circles, and legs.

And I'll be honest. I was genuinely intrigued.

I listened intently and thought, "*this is the greatest thing in the world. I'm going to be rich!*" especially after he started talking about diamonds, and rubies, and emeralds.

And it was online too! Oh, I was going to kill it!

So, I paid the $50 bucks and signed the papers, and become an IBO!

I was so excited; I couldn't wait to tell everybody that I was now an Independent Business Owner, and how I was going to become a millionaire!

Soon, I was going to all the events, which, I really enjoyed. They were high energy, filled with people from all walks of life, and they had training.

I got to network with and meet new people, and I almost always learned something new.

Now, I'm not going to name the business or the person, but if you've been around long enough, then you may know what business this is, and who that person is when you see this photo.

The following picture was taken of me, on stage during one of those events.

I was young, energetic, not 60 pounds overweight – and I was green. I was so green!

But I had the entrepreneur bug; I had that fire in me, but I didn't know the first thing about business or money.

How that played out when it came time to build that business was quite a reality check.

Picture this.

I'm driving a furniture van, moving in furniture and appliances, collecting payments, and after, when I'm all sweaty and breathing heavily after moving a refrigerator or something, I look at the customer and ask them if they're interested in a business opportunity.

I trying to book as many people as possible into meetings so I can show them "the plan" telling them how they can make some extra money, and all they had to do was change their shopping habits.

Don't laugh! It actually worked.

A lot of people responded to me, so I knew people wanted to make money, but the truth I discovered is that nobody wanted to do what I was doing to make money, so very few people signed up.

That was my first real reality check.

The second reality check came when, after months of doing this, I got my first check!

I was so happy! I had gotten the mail that day and saw the envelope. I ran inside. "*It's here! It's here! I got my first check!*" I yelled.

I tore that envelope open expecting to see big money, but what I got was $17.50.

My heart sunk. It was like someone knocked the wind out of my sails. I was talking to people every day, showing the plan, filling up the meetings, I even changed my shopping habits, for months, and after all of that, I didn't even make $20 bucks.

So, I quit and continued working my regular job.

It was humiliating hearing people ask me, "*you a millionaire yet?*" as they laughed.

The story doesn't end there though. It gets better.

A couple of weeks later, another gentleman, also older, reached out to me and wanted to meet. I knew who he was. He was the gentleman that recruited the man that recruited me.

I knew he was making good money, so I met with him for lunch, his treat, and there was another gentleman there wearing a million-dollar earner ring. I recognized it from the catalog.

He told me how the person who brought me in had quit the business, but they wanted to talk to me because I was even more active in the business than the person who signed me up was and was following the plan.

They wanted to work with me because they believed I had potential.

I looked at that million-dollar earner ring again and decided to give it another shot.

And for the next couple of months, I followed the plan. People were signing up, but I still wasn't making any real money, and then I started counting the hours.

I was making 1,000 times more money working a regular job than I was at this, so I figured I must be doing something wrong.

I decided to call my new sponsor, (he gave me his home phone), and when I called, I thought I misdialed because the person who answered said it was a distribution company.

I hung up and dialed again, and the same person answered like a distribution company. So, I asked for the gentleman, confused, and when he came to the phone, I asked him, "*I thought this was your home phone? I thought I had the wrong number.*"

He said it was his home phone.

He then explained to me that there were a few ways to make big money in that particular business and it all boiled down to sales. Move enough product and you get paid big.

After our conversation, I sat down and did the math.

Let's just say there aren't enough hours in the day for me to work the business and make the kind of money I wanted without turning my home into a distribution center too, and I was absolutely sure that I didn't want to do that.

It was a sharp reminder of the lesson I had already learned.

That is, that just because an opportunity works, it doesn't mean that people will want to do what they see someone else has to do in order to make money.

I also learned that some opportunities are so bad that you'd make more money doing what you already do.

And over the years, I've gone from one opportunity to another learning by trial and error, and when I finally figured out how to make money from home and started hitting milestones for myself and for my clients, I knew I had to share.

The milestone that inspired me to write this book was me creating a sales funnel for a client that generated just over $19,000 in three days, and the first $9,000 of it was on the very first day, within a couple of hours of one of her events.

Take a look at the next photo.

With my client's permission, I'm able to show you the latest milestone achievement on my journey to millionaire.

She hired me to build her sales funnels and she gives me free rein to design as I please. She created the assets and did the marketing, (as she should; it's her business), but I planned and built out the infrastructure for her.

The day before Thanksgiving, she asked me to build out a sales funnel, (we'll talk about what that is later), because she had an event planned, and she wanted to do a Black Friday special for after Thanksgiving.

These are the results.

She made $9,169 the day before Thanksgiving, $5,732 the day of Thanksgiving, and $4,120 the day after.

She's continued to make sales almost every day since, but what I want you to pay attention to are the summaries of the total earned for one day, and the 7 days prior.

I waited a few days to see her total sales through the whole weekend.

The number you're seeing for the last 7 days, at the time this picture was taken, began on November 25th and ended on November 30th (Cyber Monday).

How would you like to learn how to make $20,000 in 5 days?

It sounds like one of those ads you'll see on social media when you're scrolling or one of the ads you'll see if you searched for *how to make money from home*, but I assure you, it's a serious question.

In my own business I've had $1,000 days, $3,000 weekends, and so on, but between the highs and lows my income averages around $4,000 per month.

Here's what my sales look like on the back end of my system.

These are just from clients that pay me online. I have clients that cut me checks, do bank transfers, and use other means.

I'm showing you this so you can see the difference between my client's reported sales, and how I get paid by my clients because there is a difference.

I also wanted to be transparent with my earnings. My clients do make more money than me, and honestly, making them wealthy is what I get paid to do.

They should make more money than me, otherwise, they aren't getting what they paid for.

Anyway, going back to my client's earnings, she made more in a week than what my pay was per year when I worked for that rent-to-own company driving trucks.

If you do the math, $9 per hour for forty hours a week is $360 a week. $360 per week for 52 weeks is $18,720 per year.

What inspired me wasn't the money – it was helping her make the money. It was helping her get those amazing results that helped make me realize that I can't keep what I do to myself any longer.

Other people need to know how to do this because it won't be the last financial crash we have, and COVID most certainly won't be the last pandemic either if history holds true, (and it usually does).

My client is going to be able to relish making more than $10,000 in a 24-hour period, (between the 24th and 25th), and making twice that in 5 days, but I got something far more valuable, and it's going to benefit you directly.

This is proof that what I do can be duplicated by others, which to me is important because I intend to lay out a plan for you that I hope you follow, and it needs to be something that you, or anyone else for that matter, can do.

Now here is the hard truth about those numbers – what you are seeing are results.

Before you can get results like that, there is a lot that needs to happen in front of it, and a lot of learning to do. You will even try and fail a few times, so be prepared.

This is a process.

The reason I wrote this book is to help you get past many of the obstacles I've faced, so you don't have to repeat the mistakes I've made.

I want you to learn from my mistakes and learn what I've learned so that you can have success, and maybe even have it faster than I did.

Chapter 2 – The Most Important Financial Skill

Before we get into mindsets there is one more thing I need to discuss, and that is the goal of this book.

The goal of this book is to begin teaching you what I consider to be the most important financial skill anyone can develop.

> "The ability to make money from anywhere, at any time, no matter what the circumstances are."

If there is one thing I've learned from my catch-22, the economic crash, the long unemployment periods, government shutdowns, the COVID-19 pandemic, and many of the other scenarios I've run into, it is the importance of being able to make money no matter what happens.

In our lives, we prepare for every disaster and emergency, except financial ones.

Why is that?

We stock up on food and water and toilet paper. We have spare batteries, flashlights, and oil lamps. We have an emergency radio, and smoke and CO_2 detectors in our home.

First aid kits too.

We have safety drills so that we know exactly what to do in the event of the worst-case scenario.

There is a procedure for everything from escaping a burning building, to surviving a tornado, to the escape routes of a hurricane.

Why don't we have that kind of preparation so that we don't have to worry when financial disaster strikes?

There's an interesting scenario that gets played out in the form of a question in a lot of the business groups that I tend to circle around, and it begins with a question like this one.

> If someone put a gun to your head and said you have 48 hours to come up with $10,000 or I'll pull the trigger, how would you come up with the money?

I hope you're never put in that, or a similar situation, but it is an interesting question.

That question, and the various types, are brain exercises designed to get people to think about what they'd do in a serious situation.

And when you play out scenarios like that in your head, it begins the creative thinking process, and it helps you become prepared in case the worst happens.

Here's another version of that.

Imagine you lost all of your income – no more job, no family to rely on, your credit is shot – and all you have is 30 days to start over before you're evicted from your home and end up on the streets, what would you do?

By the time you're done with this book, I'm hoping that you're going to know exactly how to answer that question because you will have begun to develop what I consider to be the most important financial skill.

Chapter 3 – The Money Mindset

Mindset is one of those things that will make or break your success, guaranteed, 100% of the time, no exceptions, and it encompasses everything. Think of it as the foundation that everything gets built on.

There's this misconception though, especially in business circles that mindset is positive thinking and manifesting, and affirmations, and the law of attraction and all of that.

I mean, they have their place I guess, but that's never really served me because, at some point, all of the positive thinking and happy-happy thoughts need to be followed up by action, or nothing will come from it.

What I mean by mindset is how you think about yourself and your relationship with money.

What I mean by mindset is how you think about business and the world.

What I mean by mindset is how you view and frame problems, and obstacles, and challenges.

What I mean by mindset is how you deal with failure.

All of those things and more will not only determine if you succeed but how fast you get there, and trust me when I say that some people will be stuck in a cycle of bad mindsets for the rest of their life.

That's not a place you want to be.

Now, there is no way I can sum up all of the advice of mentors, classes, and the countless books I've learned from over the years in one book.

Instead, what I'm going to do is share the *best* mindset breakthroughs that directly helped me to start making money, and later begin to grow my income.

These were dramatic shifts in my way of thinking and had the most effect on me, and I'll start with quite possibly the biggest one.

This laid the foundation for everything else that followed.

The Big Idea: My Biggest Problem

I was several months into building an opportunity and was having very little success.

My results were mediocre at best, and I was trying just about everything I could to get more results, but nothing was working.

Frustrated, I contacted my mentor.

Now, my mentor isn't what we'd call a hand-holder, and when he speaks, he speaks plain and is sometimes blunt with the truth.

It turns some people off, but this is a quality I like about him.

During our conversation, I was hoping he could point me in the right direction and tell me what was wrong with what I was doing.

It hadn't even dawned on me that the problem was me.

Quite abruptly, he said something that changed my life!

He said,

> "Dexter. The only thing wrong with you is the six or seven inches between your ears."

I won't lie. At first, I was a little bit offended by it and a little upset, but at the same time, I really couldn't say anything back.

After our conversation ended that phrase stuck with me.

I simply couldn't let it go, and as I kept mulling it over, I realized that he was right and the journey to improve my mind began.

See, successful people don't just do things a certain way, they also think a certain way, and if I wanted to be successful too, I had to level up my thinking.

Lesson 1: Put Money in Its Rightful Place.

When it comes to the importance of money, I've found that most people either give it too much importance, or too little importance.

For some, it's all that they're about or focused on, and for others, it's *"we don't talk about money at the table"* as if it's the worst thing in the world.

For the record, money is not the root of all evil.

A lot of people habitually misquote the Bible and believe that money is evil. It's not.

The verse is 1 Timothy 6:10 and it says that it is the *love of money* that is the root of all evil.

It's the greed and the overwhelming desire that results in the things people do to get it that is the root of all evil.

It is making it the most important thing that causes the problem, and it's not.

Here is my perspective on the importance of money, and I hope this analogy makes sense as it does for me.

Question. What are the three basic needs for humans to live? And by "live", I mean life itself to be sustained.

If you said food, water, and air, you'd be correct.

We can argue shelter and be right, however, shelter isn't necessary to sustain life. We need shelter to protect us from danger and the weather, however, we're perfectly capable to survive without it given the right conditions.

Anyway, this is where it gets interesting.

The human body can live for weeks without food. I've met people who have fasted for more than 3 weeks, and research says that max, we can go for about 21 days average without eating.

We can only go a couple of days without water though, (about 3 days on average), and we can live just minutes without air.

If you were to rank food, water, and air on a scale of most important to least important, it would be pretty obvious.

Air would be the most important, followed by water, and then food.

Now, which of those three do we spend most of our time thinking about?

Food!

We spend so much time thinking about food that we have celebrity cooks with their own television shows and masterclasses. I mean we *really* think about food.

We spend most of our time thinking about the least important thing.

Why don't we think about air all the time, and it's the most important?

Unless we have breathing problems or something, we don't think about air because it's all around us, ever-present, and abundant.

Let's switch hats for a moment.

When it comes to you, what are the most important things in your life?

For me, it's my faith, my family and friends, and relationships. It's the things I love doing like music. It's my health and my time helping others.

As far as importance, money is at the very bottom of that list, and when I ask people, the vast majority of them are the same.

But what do we honestly spend most of our time thinking about?

It is money.

On average, the regular employee will spend a third of their lives on the job trying to make money, and a good portion of it commuting to and from work.

You would think with that much time in the pursuit of money that money would not be a problem, but it is.

Yet, most of the problems people have are money-related, and in fact, one of the top reasons for divorce is finance.

Money affects so much of our lives so clearly it is important.

Here's my perspective.

My goal is to make money like air.

I want money to be all around, ever-present, and abundant; not for the desire of having it, but so that I don't have to think about money, and spend my time thinking about what's important.

I don't want to spend my time thinking about the least important thing on my list of what's most important.

Now, I'll say this.

One of the most dangerous mindsets about money is that it's not important. That is the mindset of the poor.

Money is important, but not the most important thing.

You don't want to spend most of your time thinking about the least important thing, so decide to make money like air.

Think about it.

What would you do, or how would you live if you didn't have to think about money?

When you put money in its rightful place, whether you have a little or a lot, that perspective can solve a lot of problems.

This is going to sound pretentious, but if money is the most important thing to you and you're always fighting with someone about money, having the right perspective about money might be the key to saving that relationship.

All you have to do is ask yourself this question – if money weren't a problem, would we even be arguing?

You'd be surprised how many people say no.

The good news for you is that you're in a better position now to make that a reality than at any other time in history, thanks to the Internet.

Even 30 years ago it wasn't as easy as it is now, but more on that later.

Let's get into another mindset.

Lesson 2: Stop Unconsciously Repelling Money.

Another great lesson about money that I learned came from a millionaire who earned his first million in a business that I was in.

Whenever we had entrepreneurs and business owners create success, it was common practice having them coach everyone else in the business about their mindset and how they achieved their results, (their mindset, method, and mechanism – this practice is partly where the idea for the book title came from).

This particular person spoke many times, but one night in particular he taught on the topic of money, and I will never forget this lesson.

This is what he said.

> "Your bank account doesn't reflect who you are, but who you are being and your thoughts about money."

The night he spoke, the topic was about *"becoming friends with money"*.

It was all about poor mindsets, (lies and false assumptions), that we accept about money, and even though we might consciously be trying to make or acquire money, subconsciously we are sabotaging ourselves by pushing it away.

The question on the table for this lesson is, do you secretly hate money, and if you do, what can you do to become friends with money?

If you've ever wondered what makes those who succeed financially different from those who don't, or why you specifically aren't getting the results you want, somewhere in this lesson may very well be the reasons why.

WARNING: This is going to be a very uncomfortable lesson for many. It's probably going to make you very mad and make you want to stop reading, and maybe even throw something.

STOP! Keep reading, and go of all the way through the lesson, because I promise you that I will explain, and then you can make up your mind; but hear me out first.

There are three things to consider when it comes to your relationship with money and how we subconsciously repel it.

1. Personal responsibility and self-reliance. This is the one most likely to tick you off because at first, it's going to sound shocking, but hear me out.

The way I learned this was through some examples, and I'm going to share it the same way I learned it.

If I were on a job where I was being sexually harassed, or if I'm talking with someone and they say, "*you know, my boss sexually harasses me at work*," I would say, "*you know what? You need to take responsibility for that.*"

That sounds a little bit controversial, right?

If someone is in an abusive relationship, I would say to the person abused, "*you know what? You need to take responsibility for that*".

Or, if you're in a business where lots of other people are making money and you're not making money, guess what? You need to take responsibility for that.

If I said that to you, I'd sound like I'm being a jerk – but here's the thing. I'm not saying what you think I'm saying.

Check this out.

What does the word responsibility mean? Take a look at the screenshot.

responsibility

[rəˌspänsəˈbilədē]

NOUN

the state or fact of having a duty to deal with something or of having control over someone.
"a true leader takes responsibility for their team and helps them achieve goals"
synonyms: authority · control · power · leadership · management · influence · duty

- the state or fact of being accountable or to blame for something.
  "the group has claimed responsibility for a string of murders"
  synonyms: blame · fault · guilt · culpability · blameworthiness · liability
- the opportunity or ability to act independently and make decisions without authorization.
  "we would expect individuals lower down the organization to take on more responsibility"
- (responsibilities)
  a thing that one is required to do as part of a job, role, or legal obligation.
  "he will take over the responsibilities of overseas director"
  synonyms: duty · task · function · job · role · place · charge · business · onus · burden · liability · accountability · answerability · province · pigeon
- (responsibility to/toward)
  a moral obligation to behave correctly toward or in respect of.
  "individuals have a responsibility to control personal behavior"
  synonyms: trustworthiness · level-headedness · rationality · sanity · reason · reasonableness · sense · common sense · stability · maturity · adultness · reliability · dependability · competence

Everyone knows one of the sub-definitions pretty well. That is being accountable or to blame for something, and sadly, a lot of people think it *only* means blame, and who's fault is it.

That's just how society thinks in general.

So, for example, let's say people see something bad happening on the news, the first thing they tend to think about is who's fault is it, and who's to blame.

They want to hold someone accountable for it, but that's not all responsibility means.

There are other definitions too that are very important.

They are:

1. *The opportunity or ability to act independently and make decisions without authorization.*
2. *A moral obligation to behave correctly toward or in respect of.*

As a third meaning, it also means *a thing that is required to do as part of a job, role, or legal obligation*, meaning to "take responsibility" over something that has to be done in order to do something else.

Fault and blame are actually negative things, and also victimhood-type of concepts, so let's push that aside for a moment and focus on the other definitions.

Responsibility, how it's applied here, simply means you have the ability to respond.

So, if someone's in an abusive relationship, and I tell them they have to take responsibility for that, I'm not saying it's their fault, or that they're to blame for the situation.

I'm saying they have the ability to respond and they have a duty to take responsibility for changing their lives and getting out of that situation.

They have to take ownership of that situation and reserve for themselves the ability to respond, whether it means getting help from friends, going to the police, going to therapy, or counseling, and so on, and they don't need anyone's permission or authorization to do that.

In fact, the best thing you can do for yourself is to forget about blame and fault because they rarely ever serve a good purpose.

Here are some other examples that I've heard, and maybe you have too.

Some people want to blame McDonalds® for people being overweight. Some want to blame Wall Street or the Federal Reserve for somebody else being broke.

Others want to blame Coca Cola® for children getting diabetes.

Yes, that is responsibility, but it's all fault and blame. It has nothing to do with you creating results for yourself.

Fault and blame are not attributes of excellence and personal production, whereas personal responsibility and self-reliance are.

So, maybe Coca Cola® has products that aren't in our best interest. Maybe McDonalds® is making cheap food that does cause people to be overweight, but what's your stake in it?

At what point do we take personal responsibility for our actions?

Nobody has put a gun to anyone's head and is forcing them to consume those products.

So, you have to take ownership of your situation and reserve for yourself the ability to respond, because at the end of the day, no matter who is at fault or to blame, **you are where you are in your life because of your best thinking**.

That's a big concept, so let me explain it.

Your life is going the way it is because of the choices in life you've made, meaning that your best thinking got you to where you are now.

Think about it.

All of our lives, we've made decisions, and usually, it's the best decision we can make right then and there. That means your life is the way it is as a result of your best thinking.

A lot of people have a long list of reasons why their life isn't working.

For example, my boss wouldn't give me a raise, I can't get overtime hours, gas prices are too high, nobody is giving me the break I need, the Republicans, the Democrats, the rich, immigrants, the patriarchy.

I was one of those people. I had a list too, but guess what? I wasn't on that list.

It was everyone and everything else's fault but my own for how my life was going.

I had to take responsibility for my life, and so will you if you're ever going to see the change you want to see.

Think about this too.

When you see other people, who are just like you, but are doing better than you are, you have to consider that they're operating in the same economy that you are.

They have the same president as you. They have the same congress as you. They pay the same prices at the pump – why is it that they're doing better?

Once you decide to stop going through the motions of mediocrity in your life and commit to doing whatever you can, from where you are, with what you've got, you'll start seeing results.

I don't know exactly why that happens, but it's happened in my life too.

When you decide to take personal responsibility and become self-reliant, even if nothing else externally changes, you'll see results.

I was also taught that *the life you want also wants you*, but the only way you'll get it is to stop pretending that your results in life have anything to do with external factors.

They don't.

2. You need to make friends with money. This too is a bit controversial, but it needs to be said.

Some people want to get rich, but they won't say that because it's not a polite or 'politically correct' thing to say, and as a result of not saying what they really want, they've been keeping money at arm's length, and have been all of their working lives.

Here's a thought question.

Have you ever stopped and truly asked yourself why there isn't money flowing into your life?

Follow me here.

People who like something tend to have a lot of it in their lives.

People who like art, have a lot of art in their house. People who like cars have a lot of cars in their garages. If you like dogs, you probably have a lot of dogs.

People who like to travel, probably go on a lot of trips. People who like fashion, probably have tons of clothes and other apparel.

That's how people are.

We tend to invest in and bring into our lives the things we like. So, guess what?

People who like money… They probably have a lot of money.

If you want money but don't have it flowing into your life, you have to ask yourself why. Given that everything else is largely the same, (gas prices, the president, the economy…), what makes "them" different from you?

There are two main reasons why you don't have wealth.

1. You never actually decided to be wealthy. Becoming wealthy is not accidental. People don't just accidentally stumble and fall into being rich. That is extremely rare.

   Even if you had a million-dollar idea, you still have to put in the work to make that idea a reality and turn it into something major.

   Most people are content to just "make ends meet" and "have enough" to get by.

2. You really don't like money all that much. More than that, some are scared of it, they're negative about it, and as a result, they repel it from them.

Here's the thing though.

People need money. They want money and work hard to get money, so how do they repel it?

One of the ways is by not admitting what it is they want. They'll sugar coat it mentally because of a bad mindset, usually about a word, in this instance, the word rich.

See, a lot of people want to be rich, but they won't speak aloud the word rich.

They say that they want to be "financially independent," or "financially free," or even "financially successful".

They'll say everything but what it is they truly want, even though they mean the same thing. Rich and wealthy mean the same thing. Rich and financially independent mean the same thing.

Why won't someone just come out and say, "*I want to be rich*"?

Just think about how your friends would react if everyone were talking about what they want for their lives and you say you want to be rich.

Think about all the things we, as a culture, admire in others.

If someone were to say they wanted to be emotionally healthy, let go of past hurts and wrongs, forgive, and heal so they could be better people, we'd cheer for that. That's just admirable.

If someone were to say they wanted to be as physically healthy as they can be, stop eating junk, and begin working out to be healthier for themselves and those they love, we'd for that. It's a noble thing.

If someone were to say that they wanted to become more intellectually healthy and stop watching junk television and start reading more, and bettering themselves, we'd cheer that too.

Tell someone that you want to be as financially healthy as possible though, and have an abundance of money coming in, to travel freely and have nice things, and have a lifestyle that most people only dream about, and it tends to be viewed as greed and selfishness.

Have you ever asked yourself why certain topics like politics, religion, and money tend to be slightly more taboo than all the others?

Granted, this tends to be a kind of Western mindset, however, I've met many people who had a house rule whenever I brought up any of those topics.

I'd start talking about either of those only to find myself cut off to, "*three things we don't talk about in this house. Money, politics, and religion,*" or some other similar sentiment.

That sentiment has two underlying beliefs.

1. The belief that money isn't important.
2. The belief that people must choose between money and something else.

Regarding the importance of money, we already talked about putting money in the right perspective. Money is important.

It's just as important as the food it buys, the medicine it buys, the clothes that it buys, and everything else it buys to have a life.

Regarding the second, this is the most dangerous of the two because how you think about money is important, and a lot of people believe this lie, that they can't have money and whatever else they consider important.

I'll prove it to you. I'll say a phrase and all you have to do is fill in the blank.

"We might not have a lot of money, but at least we're _____".

You already knew how to fill in the bank, didn't you? We've all heard someone say something like that, and honestly, it sounds like the right thing to say.

Fill in the blank. What are some of the things you've heard people say?

Here are some of mine.

We might not have a lot of money, but at least we're happy. We might not have a lot of money, but at least we're honest. We might not have a lot of money, but at least we love God.

And people say it as if having money has anything to do with happiness, honesty, loving your family, loving God, or anything else.

Some people actually believe that having a lot of money makes them bad people, and when they see rich people, they get mad.

I and some friends were hanging out and talking on the front porch one day, and one of my neighbors had a visitor driving a very expensive car.

We notice it and started talking about it because we've rarely ever seen one. While we're talking about it, admiring the car, thinking about asking the visitor if he could take us for a ride, one of my friends said this.

"… yeah. I wonder how many people he had to rip off to get that car."

He said it with such disgust too and it turned into an argument when another friend asked, *"who said he had to rip anyone off? He could be an honest person,"* and it went from there.

The point is, can you see why a person with this belief about money would be working hard to make money, but it's not quite working for them?

Their belief system won't allow them to succeed.

Our brains are hardwired in such a way that it fulfills our beliefs. It's built for survival.

There is a whole, long explanation of what we call the self-fulfilling prophesy that we can get into, (and maybe I will), but what you need to know is that what you believe is what determines your outcome.

So, if a person tells themselves that they don't have a lot of money, but at least they're happy, or honest, or loves their family, or they're a good Christian, or any of the other ways they would fill in the blank, what they've done is programmed their brain in such a way that being poor or being broke is a part of their identity.

They believe that to love their kids, or go to church, or be a good person, and so on, is to not have a lot of money, and no matter how hard they work for it, that survival mechanism in their brain won't let them have the results that they're filling in the blank with.

They will subconsciously repel money faster than they can possibly imagine.

I have learned this firsthand to be true, and if you remember at the start of the book, it was one of the most important lessons I've ever learned.

> "Dexter. The only thing wrong with you is the six or seven inches between your ears."

Believe me when I tell you this. If you do not get your mindset right; if you don't get the six or seven inches between your ears working properly, you will not ever get the results you want.

And it starts with real self-improvement, and it starts with learning about money and how it works.

3. Disconnect in your head any relationship you have between money and time. It may seem like a strange thing to ask, but it's really important that you get this.

Some people are repelling money because they don't believe they deserve it, and it has to do with how society works.

In Western culture, there is a kind of deservedness that's associated with working hard your entire life to "make an honest living", and for a lot of people, those who make money quickly without working for it; it's almost like they didn't earn it.

We see it with lottery winners. They have what's called winner's gilt. It's where a person who's worked hard for everything their entire life, suddenly comes into a lot of money that they didn't work for, and they'll feel guilty, oftentimes giving their money away.

This was something I had to overcome, and something my family had to overcome too because when I decided that I was going to make money in a way that goes against the social grain, it feels kind of like cheating.

For example, my parents are the hardest working people I've ever met, and they worked their entire lives to take care of me and my sisters, but they never figured out how money really works.

And by that, I don't mean how to save, budget, or pay taxes. They were actually very good at making the most out of the money they earned.

What I mean is that they never figured out how to make money without trading time for it, and when I started having $1,000 days and $3,000 weekends, they were happy for me and proud of me, but they didn't understand it.

Because they didn't understand how I can make that kind of money from home, it was almost like I didn't earn that money; not really.

Even when the checks were coming in, I'd hear *"if you want to make money, get a job"*.

The plan my family had for me was to get a job and this "Internet thing you're doing" should be to supplement your job income, and the standard line of attack, when they were upset with me was, *"go out and get a real job"*.

I used to get mad when they said stuff like that, but I didn't after a while, because I understood that they didn't understand that time and money don't really have anything to do with each other.

Trading time for money is only one way of making money; the other way is to trade value.

And when you truly understand that you can sit at home with a laptop, and make $1,000 in a day, or $3,000 in a weekend, or make money while you're sleeping, it changes your life.

For me, it meant that I didn't have to wake up at the crack of dawn, drag myself out of bed, commute to a job that barely paid me enough to get by, only to come home at the end of the day exhausted.

You need to know that it's okay to be rich.

It's okay to make a lot of money and not have to work tirelessly, spending most of your time at a job trying to build a "life you can hang your hat on".

You don't deserve money any less for making it in 2 hours, than if it took you 2 months.

It really is okay to get rich.

Now, here's the thing – I believe that it's okay to be rich if you do so being at the service of people.

There are two ways to make money; at the expense of others, and in the service of others.

Don't ever make your money at the expense of people. I believe in this full-heartedly.

I make my money by being of value and service to other people. I help solve problems and make people's lives easier. I love being of service to others.

This is how I choose to make money.

I don't trade time for money; I trade value for money, and any time I spend in business it's either to create value or get customers.

If there's anything you take from this lesson, it's this:

1. It's okay to be rich. In fact, in one of the next lessons we're going to do some math that will show you that it's absolutely necessary.
2. You deserve to be rich, meaning everyone deserves to live the best life they possibly can, and if you're a provider, so do the people in your charge, especially family. It is your duty to provide the life your family deserves if that is your role.
3. Gain that wealth by being of value and service to others, because how you make money matters, especially if you're to understand free enterprise properly, (and most don't).

So, let's talk about free enterprise.

Lesson 3: Understand Free Enterprise (Properly).

Free enterprise, to the average person, is largely misunderstood and often perceived in a negative light because most average people have a poverty mindset, although I'm sure they don't see it that way.

I didn't. I thought I was being an honest person.

When I truly understood free enterprise properly though it changed my life and my views about money, and I'm sure it will yours as well.

Putting aside the economical discussions and the politics, (both are irrelevant to this application), the mechanics of free enterprise offers a unique perspective on money that I highly recommend people adopt.

That premise is this:

I'm not getting paid for my time. I'm getting paid for the value that I give to other people.

Why would someone pay $9,000 or $10,000 for a Rolex® watch that doesn't tell time any better than the $150 Casio® on my wrist? In fact, as accuracy goes, the digital clock on my cell phone is probably more accurate.

Why would someone buy a high-end pen like a Montblanc® ink pen for anywhere from $400 to $1,000, when it writes just as well as a $5.00 pen from an office supplies store?

Or why do some people drive a $100,000 car when a $20,000 car would do the same thing, especially since some cheaper cars pack more features in to make it more comfortable?

Why do people wear Nike® instead of a $30 pair of shoes from a Payless®?

To understand why you have to understand what free enterprise is.

Let's say you went to Office Max® and bought a Parker® pen for $35, and on a trip somewhere, you and I run into each other, got to talking, and decided to trade information.

As you're writing down your information, I see you pull out the pen and all of a sudden, I'm awestruck. I say, "*Is that a Parker pen? Can I see it?*"

You hand it over for me to look at, and after I do, I decided that I wanted to buy it from you, and I say, "*I will pay you $500 for the pen right now*".

So, you paid $35 for a pen, and I want it, and offer you $500 for it.

Why on Earth would I do that?

So, you ask, "*why on Earth would you pay me $500 for a pen?*"

Now, what if I said that I collect Parker® pens and that pen actually went out of production and I can't find one anywhere else, and I need it to complete my collection.

Hold that thought.

How would feel if that happened? What would be going through your mind?

Would you feel like you're taking advantage of me if you take my $500?

Some people would just tell me to take it and make it a gift. I've been in a similar situation with something else and that's what the person wanted to do.

They didn't want to take my money because they thought they were taking advantage of me, and they made it a gift because they wanted to be altruistic.

As noble as that might seem, that's a deservedness issue.

37

Some people put themselves in a situation where they are giving away a lot of stuff or not accepting money for things because, in reality, they're scared of money.

I'm not saying don't give gifts. It's good to give gifts.

I'm saying don't ever give gifts when it's a symptom of poverty consciousness. You've got to take responsibility for that and deal with it.

Some people would say, *"you know what? I only paid $35 for it. Just give me $35 for it and call it even. I'd feel bad if I took $500"*.

I think most people are in that category, and I've run into this situation as well. They were just good, average people, and here's the truth.

Good, average people never get rich; that's why they're called average.

Now, being average is not good, bad, right, or wrong. You're free to live your life how you see fit, but the truth is that average people generally do not become rich.

Going back to the scenario, let's say you decided to say, *"Yes. I'll take the $500,"* then you deserve that. You deserve the $465 profit.

Some will think it's unfair, but fair is whatever two people agree on as being fair.

An offer was made, you and I both agreed, and an exchange was made. You earned that money. You deserve that profit.

It's called the law of equivalent exchange, (or the law of fair exchange), and without going into a long explanation, it essentially means that we're not really moving products and services, or money back and forth.

Those are just objects being exchanged. What we're actually exchanging is value.

I'm moving a certain amount of value that I own, and you're giving me a certain amount of value that you own, and we're making an exchange.

It can be money, time, resources, advice, products, services, entertainment, and more.

For example, when you work a traditional job, you're exchanging something of value to you, (your time), for something of value to the company, (their money). The company made an offer, (pay or salary), and when you were hired you both agreed, and the exchange began.

In the case of our $35 pen, I placed your pen's value to be at least $500, probably more, because I'm getting a bargain.

My now-completed pen set will be worth a few thousand dollars, and I will have only paid $500 to complete that set.

And if I value your pen at $500, how much you paid for it doesn't matter, does it? It's irrelevant to the offer, as are the materials in the pen.

I say that because something a lot of people do is try to break down how something is made and base value on it. It's actually quite common.

Here's another example.

Let's say you were outside working all morning, mowing the lawn, raking leaves, pulling weeds from the garden, and so on.

Now, you're hot and thirsty.

Just across the street from you, the neighbor's kid daughter set up a stand selling ice-cold, home-made lemonade, and was charging $1.00 for a cup.

Are you going to whip out a calculator and a scale and try to figure out how many ounces of lemon juice is in a cup, or the cost of lemons, and all of that?

Of course not.

She's selling you a cup that probably has 10 cents in it, but you're happy to give her the $1.00 because you value the lemonade. You're hot and thirsty. The value to you is worth the exchange of the $1.00 she's asking.

Or how about this?

You think that your wife might be pregnant. You come home from work or you're having dinner and your daughter says, "*I think I might be pregnant*".

After the surprise passes, you decide that it's important to know for sure, so you go to the store and decide you want the best, most accurate pregnancy test, so you leave nothing to chance.

So, you look at the option and see the test is $38.

Now, if you've ever seen a pregnancy test, you'll know that it's nothing but a chemical strip and reacts to the hormones present in a woman's body and tell you yes or no, depending on whether they are present or not. It's nothing super fancy.

It's a chemical strip, molded plastic, and a little bit of formatted plastic for the screen, designed in such a way so that it tells you yes or no, or indicates with a plus or minus sign, or bars, etc.

Here's the question.

Did you just buy some plastic with a chemical strip in it? No. You didn't.

I want you to think like a merchant and not a consumer. What were you paying for?

You were paying for the answer to a very important, emotional question. Are we pregnant?

That's what free enterprise is.

The company that sold a $38 pregnancy kit earned and deserved every penny they made. They earned and deserved their cut of the profit in that transaction because they assisted you in getting you what you wanted – the answer to the question.

So, I put it forward to you that people who make their money being of service to others, by providing solutions and answering questions, both earn and deserve every penny they make because of who they serve and even changed lives.

If you become rich being in service to others, then you earn and deserve that wealth.

In my industry, I teach people different ways to make money, as well as how to make money working from home.

Their success stories are why I can say that I earn and deserve the money I make, and when I hear stories of others who do it and the results, they earned theirs too.

For example, hearing about a dad who no longer has to work two jobs, because he figured out how to make more money doing what he was already doing. That's service.

When I hear about a single mom who's able to pay all the bills and not have to worry about whether or not her deadbeat ex is going to pay child support this month. That's service.

There are a lot of examples of people changing their lives in our industry.

The college kid who doesn't have to worry about student loans piling up because he learned how to make extra money turning a hobby into a little side hustle that pays well.

That husband and wife who has a daughter getting ready for prom and a son that needs new uniforms and an instrument, and they don't have to pick and choose what gets sacrificed to make both happen.

Or how about this?

The man and wife whose daughter is getting married soon, planning a wedding, and they realize they can't afford to take their guests to Burger King®, let alone pay for catering.

That and more comes as a result of being in service to others. Even more than that, I'm very proud when my clients and customers leave reviews of myself and my work.

I love helping people, and there is such personal satisfaction there for me.

But here's the thing.

It starts with you being self-reliant. It starts with you taking personal responsibility. It starts with deciding to not live like a victim anymore.

There's a saying that I'm very fond of. *"My life is not happening to me; I'm happening to my life and I better start making some moves"*.

In other words, I'm going to reserve for myself the ability to respond. Fault and blame don't matter.

A leader is someone who accepts responsibility whether it's his/her fault or not, and if I am to be a leader, then I have to do the same.

Once you do that, become friends with money, and make your money being of service and value to people, and not at the expense of them.

See, you deserve to be rich, not just because of yourself, but because of those who rely on you. Your family deserves the best life you can provide for them.

It has nothing to do with how hard you work. It has nothing to do with how much time you put in. It's okay for you to want to be rich.

You don't need anyone's permission to make a lot of money and live your best life, and if you do, then I give you permission.

See, I learned that a lot of people make fun of the rich because they can't afford what the rich have. It's a kind of mental defense. It's like that conversation I and my friends had.

We're all thinking about how nice it would be to have one, and my friend is puffed up with pride, assuming that the guy with the nice car is some capitalist pig who took advantage of people – meanwhile, he's still figuring out how to afford new tires for his broke-mobile.

Do you want to know why Bill Gates is rich? Look at the people he's served. He invented software that's probably sitting on your desk right now. Or Jeff Bezos who employs almost a million people helping to keep the lights on and food on the table for their families.

If you want to make more money, be of more service.

Discussion.
Is your head hurting yet?

When I teach people what you've just learned, more than a few have said that their heads hurt. These are big concepts to understand, let alone mindsets to adopt as an adult because you were raised at a disadvantage.

By that I mean the disadvantage of knowledge most people have when they're not raised in wealth. The rich pass on knowledge to their children from a very young age, because it is expected of them to maintain and grow the wealth they are left.

That's how wealth becomes generational.

If you weren't raised in that environment, not only are you missing the information the rich pass on to their kids, but you were raised with the understanding of the other side of the wealth coin – poverty.

In essence, you might have been raised to carry on generational poverty and you may not even realize it. Some even defend it.

This goes back to deservedness issues when you hear stories about generations of people working hard their entire lives to eke out a living, and they're proud of having a history of their grandparents and parents working hard to build a life, and it's what they're doing now, and want their kids to do as well.

With exception to family businesses, this is one of the ways poverty becomes generational.

And if you're hearing any of this for the first time or have never had this explained in such a way, then it's quite possible that you'll get a headache or two, but now that you know, the whole world just changed for you.

This is how money works all around the world, and has always worked, and will probably always work. When the first humans began trading goods with each other to survive, to the barter systems of the past, to the present where money and transactions are 1s and 0s in accounts traveling the information superhighway it was, is, and will be all about value.

It is all value exchange, and the people who create real, lasting wealth think a certain way.

The implications of understanding how money actually works in our world and why things are the way they are is quite profound, and there are discussions to be had in all aspects of our society.

The advantage you have now is that you live in a time where you can learn this from a book.

I've lost count of how many masterminds I've had to be involved in to learn this stuff. Not just masterminds either, but seminars, online classes, mentors, and coaches too.

Some required money, others required me to join businesses to get access, and all of them required time.

Remember that you're not trading money. You are trading value.

Chapter 4 – Money & Mindset Lessons

In chapter 2 you learned about the most important financial skill, and in chapter 3 you learned about the money mindset.

In this chapter, we're going to build on that with a series of smaller mindsets that probably wouldn't otherwise make complete sense without the foundation of the first two chapters.

Because there are so many, these will be relatively short, but I will take the time to explain each of them, and hopefully, they'll be easy to understand.

Lesson 1: Stop Caring Where Your Money Comes From.

One of the hurdles I had to cross on my journey from working traditional jobs to working full time at home was to understand that it didn't matter where my money came from as long as it was legal and ethical.

Some people falsely believe that if money isn't made a certain way, then it's bad money.

For example, when people told me, *"You want to make money? Get a job,"* that is a false belief. It's only one way to make money.

I personally know some people who believe that the only way to make "real" money is to start a brick-and-mortar company. That's false too.

Again, it's only one way to make money.

The truth is that there are many ways to make money and I think a lot of people have a sense of pride that won't let them see it or do it if they do see it.

That was my problem.

I'm an accomplished musician and classical composer, as well as a programmer and network engineer. After the 2008/2009 crash, I couldn't find work in my career field at all, and the work I did find were jobs I swore I'd never go back to, like being a convenient store clerk or working security.

And then there were jobs that I outright thought were beneath me, like cutting grass, painting houses, and farm work. I've done all of those jobs before, but once I had my education and training, I felt I shouldn't have to go back to them.

I'm not proud of who I was then because I was a prideful idiot.

Money is money, and I had to learn that as long as it's earned legally and ethically, it doesn't matter what the work is. You do what you have to do.

Pride doesn't pay the bills and it doesn't put food on the table, and a foreclosure notice doesn't care if you're feeling embarrassed to be seen working at a job you think is below you.

What's important to remember though is that what you choose to do as work doesn't have to be a career decision. A lot of jobs especially today will be, and probably should be, temporary.

I did a lot of odd jobs to raise money to get my business started while I was learning to work from home; jobs I never wanted to do and even looked down on.

Hindsight is 20/20 though, and looking back, if I didn't forget my pride and stopped caring where my money came from, I wouldn't be where I am now working from home and writing this book.

On the other side of jobs people won't do because of pride, there are ways to make money that people won't do because of offense.

Some people think out of a poor mindset that some work is too sleazy or dirty. For example, sales, or stock brokering.

Thanks to modern culture, some ways of money just trigger our sensibilities about what's right or wrong.

I've heard people swear off entire professions as well. They'll say things like, *"Ugh! I'll never be a defense attorney. I would never defend criminals."*

Both sides of that coin, whether it's pride or offense, stem from a poor mindset about money, and the sooner I was able to get over that mindset, the more opportunities there were for me to prosper.

Sometimes you have to do what you need to do today to create a stepping-stone to get where you want to be tomorrow, and you can't let pride or offense stop you from achieving your goals.

Stop caring where your money comes from. You'll be surprised at how many opportunities there really are around you.

But before you run out the door and start looking for a handyman job, make sure and read the next lesson.

Lesson 2: Multiple Streams of Income the Smart Way.

There was a saying that one of my mentors said repeatedly, and it's always stuck with me.

> "Millionaires are millionaires because they find two or three ways of making money, doing what they already do."

Most people rightfully take that to mean creating multiple streams of income but end up trying to do two or three different things related to what they're doing to create income streams.

I can't tell you how many aspiring entrepreneurs I've met who were struggling because they were trying to make two or three different opportunities work together.

Even though they might have been affiliate programs, for example, and they were all in the same market, they were independent of each other, the person was trying to create a system where their customers had to buy several products from different companies.

There isn't anything wrong that if the products complement each other and can help the customer achieve their goal, but it has to be a logical progression and make sense for it to work.

What I think though, is that people who do that miss the actual point. There is a bigger meaning behind that lesson when one considers the part of *"doing what they already do"*.

It means you can turn what you're already doing into multiple streams of income without having to start two or three new and/or different things.

For example, if you're a construction worker you may have picked up some tips, tricks, and little-known information that others don't know about and could probably use. Maybe you even have a specialty.

You could take that knowledge and turn it into multiple streams of income.

You could write guides for new construction workers to help them make the job easier, or you could consult on jobs where your expertise was valuable.

You could make tutorial videos with tips or tricks that would save others time, or you could teach a course on your specialization, all while holding down your regular job.

And with the strategy, (the method), and the right tools and resources, (the mechanism), you could have three or four streams of income, all while holding down your regular job, and without having to put out much more time.

This is one of the best ways to create additional income, especially if you're a busy person.

Later on, when we talk about mechanisms, you'll have the opportunity to flesh out this idea in more detail, even get started on the path to creating additional income streams.

Lesson 3: Sweat Equity Is Just as Valuable as Money, If Not More.

Have you heard the saying, *"It takes money to make money"*? As far as truth goes, it's a partial truth. It's kind of like the saying, *"if you want to make money, get a job"*.

Yes, you can use money to make money, but you don't <u>have</u> to have money in order to get started with creating income streams.

As one of my high school science teachers, Ms. Plewes, used to say, *"Sometimes all you need is a little bit of elbow grease"*. She was speaking about sweat equity or good old-fashioned hard work.

When I re-started my IT company, I was coming off of a financial crash, and having been out of work for about 18 months, I was dead broke.

Yet, I was able to start a successful PC repair business and grow it into the tech company I have today.

How did I do that? How does one go from dead broke, relying on family to eat, to starting a company with no money?

It was actually quite simple.

First, I cleared out our garage and set up tables so I would have a place to work.

Then, I mowed some lawns and did a couple of odd jobs for people, and used the money to print up flyers I had designed on an old laptop computer.

Then, I and my dad walked for miles passing out those flyers all over our neighborhood.

I used the money from the first PC repair job I did to buy materials for my dad to make a sign that sat in our front yard for years.

He and I continued to make flyers and walk around passing them out.

Eventually, I learned how to market online properly and started taking advantage of free services to promote my business. The more I learned, the more I implemented, and the more my company grew.

I never liked the phrase, *"it takes money to make money"*. It always seemed incomplete to me, or at least misleading.

The truth I discovered is that takes money to operate a business and it takes money to *grow* money, but it doesn't take money to start making money.

So, don't get hung up on not having money to get started doing something.

Many times, the fastest path to getting started is just being willing to put out some elbow grease.

Lesson 4: It's Not About the Hustle. It's About the Gains.

I love a hustler. They go hard all day and they're about their business 24/7, no-nonsense, get it done, and keep going.

Hustle builds momentum. Hustle gets fast results. Hustle makes things happen.

But hustle without consistency is a chaotic frenzy, and ultimately a losing game.

One of the most important things I've learned about building wealth is that it is built over time. Getting rich overnight rarely happens, and few who gain it rarely stay rich.

From experience, when I've heard stories about people who achieved great financial wealth, it was always about what's in the news or about some major event.

For example, a few years ago, in one of the businesses I was in, there was an affiliate who joined the business and in a matter of months, he went from starting out to making over a million dollars.

There were two basic reactions to that; some attributed it to luck, and everyone wanted to know how he became an overnight success.

So, one day, he taught his strategy to all of us, and it turns out he wasn't an overnight success at all. It turns out that he brought a lot into the business with him and joining the business was just a way to capitalize on what he was already doing.

He had years and years of knowledge working for him, resources he had built up, as well as systems and processes it took him years to design and build so he could go into any opportunity and become massively successful in a very short time.

See, there really isn't anything such as overnight success, and when I forget about the events and news people are talking about and dig deeper into the stories of the people who achieved the result, you'll discover that money is an end result.

You'll discover, as I did, that success is built on a road of hard work and consistency.

I learned that the hard way and it was another mentor, who in no uncertain terms made it clear that inconsistency was my problem.

He said, *"Dexter. You're all hustle and no flow"*.

You have to put in the work consistently, whether it's for an hour or two every day, or five to ten hours a week.

That time adds up, and your work will compound.

How I dealt with my inconsistency was forcing myself to use a schedule. I'd block out time on my calendar just to work on my businesses.

I gave up watching television and movies for a while to have more time for myself, and I also created rewards for myself when I met goals.

So, let's say that I got something done that I'd normally procrastinate on? I'd reward myself with the freedom to watch a movie and have a really nice meal.

I also found an accountability partner that pushed me to get things done when I fell off, and I put her in control of the rewards so I couldn't cheat myself.

I'm not saying this is something you should do, but if you have an inconsistency problem, this is what worked for me, and I'd recommend trying it out and see how it works.

Bottom line? Be consistent. Hustle alone won't get you where you want.

Lesson 5: Failure Isn't Failure If You Fail Forward.

The story of Chester Carlton, (the inventor of Xerox), is probably one of the greatest success stories of perseverance there is in business.

I won't go into the full story but up until he invented Xerox, how the world made copies was very different and very messy.

See, back then to make a copy you had to physically place carbon paper between two sheets of paper so that whatever you wrote or typed on the first would be copied to the second.

And for as many copies as you needed you had to repeat this process.

Carlton decided that he didn't like doing that and sought to change it.

He conducted chemical experiments in his own home, much to the disapproval of his wife, who eventually divorced him. The chemicals smelled really bad, and to hear the stories, his wife allegedly said that he was like a child playing with colors.

Still, he persisted, and after many failures, in 1938 he printed his first copy.

You would think that this alone would be revolutionary, but between 1939 and 1944, 20 companies turned him down for production including IBM.

Had he not persisted, there's no telling as to where we would be. The invention of Xerox inspired digital printing itself.

As much as this is a story of persistence, there is a greater lesson that can be extracted from this regarding failure and how you deal with it.

After failing a few times, or failing at something for a long time, most people quit and move on to the next thing.

This is natural human behavior to some degree, but it is also a choice.

In Carlton's story, before we get to his first successful print, there were countless attempts and failures every step of the way, but he didn't regard them as failures.

As I studied his work and saw his diagrams leading up to the Xerox 914, (the first commercial copier), he laid out each step was a progression on the last one.

He made it a point to learn from his mistakes and either correct them or avoid them completely, and when you look at failure from that perspective, success is all but inevitable.

In fact, much of the work towards creating success begins with a foundation of avoiding and correcting mistakes, because as you do, you're that much closer to achieving your goal.

You'd be surprised how many people succeed simply by not repeating mistakes.

I learned that avoiding mistakes and learning from failure is progress.

I learned that when I fail, before I decide to let it go, I put in the time and break it down and try to determine why I failed and what I can do to either learn from it or fix it.

I ask myself analytical questions like, is it avoidable? Is there another way to do that one thing as opposed to starting over? Is there a way to avoid this broken step entirely?

If everything up to a point works, getting past the point where it stops working really is the only obstacle I have, and putting in a little extra time to learn from it at the very least makes it less likely I'll fail to that thing again.

I would tell anyone that doing the same is well worth the effort because if you can solve or avoid one small problem, it is far better to do that than start over.

Failure is a part of success. Embrace it, and learn from it.

Lesson 6: Profit Is An End Result, Not A Goal.

The day that I knew I had to do something else was a very hard day for me. It was emotionally turbulent and I was wracked with all kinds of conflicting thoughts.

I was on a job I hated, in a situation I hated, working alongside people that didn't like me, had a bully for a supervisor, and even though I was good at my job, it was a very hostile work environment.

Just to get to the job I had to drive about 2 hours one way, and pay for parking. I got home very late at night and didn't even come close to getting enough sleep.

On top of that, I was always broke. It seemed like I only had enough money to pay for gas to get to and from work.

That day, everything came to a head as I sat there in a parking lot, with what seemed like an existential question.

I had spent too much money on gas and food and forgot to hold back enough money to pay for parking, and was trying to decide whether I should just go home and miss a day of work, or risk going to work and getting the vehicle towed.

The longer I sat there the angrier I became, mostly at myself, as did the anxiety of trying to decide whether to call it a day or take a risk at being stranded.

And, in one painful moment it all finally came out and I burst into tears. I had enough. I was done, and I said audibly, with tears in my eyes, *"I can't do this shit for the rest of my life"*, and I quit.

I started up the van, pulled out of the parking lot, and left.

I was so stressed out that I passed the exit ramp to go home three times and had to keep turning around.

I went home expecting to get yelled at because I didn't have a fallback plan. I didn't have another job lined up and I didn't even know what I was going to do next, and to my surprise, everyone understood and left me alone.

It was on that backdrop that I decided that I had to become a business owner; an entrepreneur and the goal was to make money.

I *had* to be profitable because it was the only way I would never have to work another job like that ever again. It was the only way out of commuting, and I hated commuting with a passion at that point.

As I continued to work other jobs, (had to pay the bills) and learned about business, I somehow forgot that the whole reason I was in business was to create a lifestyle for myself.

It was drilled into my head that the goal of every business is to make a profit, and eventually, I learned that that way of thinking was wrong.

I learned that profit was the end result of running a successful business.

More to the point, profit is what happens when there is an exchange of value, and the best value will be the value that is in the service of others, helping them to achieve their goals, solve problems, or make their lives easier.

In his book *Secrets of Closing the Sale*, Zig Ziglar is quoted as saying, *"You can have everything in life you want if you will just help enough other people get what they want"*.

I believe that, and to me, the goal of business is to serve others first and foremost.

Lesson 7: Value Equals Profit. More Value Equals More Profit.

Once I understood that the goal of business is to serve, value took on a whole new meaning, because the profit I made was a direct result of how much value I offered, both actual and perceived.

I stopped thinking about the world in terms of money and started thinking about the world in terms of value.

What problems can I solve? How can I help others get what they want?

How can I make someone's life easier or better?

I started looking for problems to solve and finding ways to solve them, and it changed everything for me because everywhere I looked there were people with problems that needed help!

The world is filled with opportunities, and if you can find a way to help someone else, you can make a lot of money.

Before I understood this, finding, or creating opportunities was a very hard thing to do, because the focus was on how to get money from someone.

The problem was that once I got their money, I had to ask, why would they give me money again, or give me money every month, and then I'd have to essentially start over trying to hard sell to new people.

That is a lot of work!

Now, value can be actual or perceived. What's the difference?

Actual value is how much something is worth or the price. For example, let's say you buy a car for $35,000. That's what that is worth at the time you bought it. That's the price.

Perceived value would be how much that car would be worth to you after you've had it for a while, and it means a lot to you. We call that sentimental value.

Or, when you're shopping and you see a bargain, you feel like you're getting more from that bargain than the amount of money you're paying for it.

In other words, the perceived value is higher than the amount of money on the price tag, and a good salesperson, no matter how much the asking price, will deliver more value, actual or perceived, than the money the customer has to pay.

Remember the law of equivalent exchange? We aren't trading products for money. We are exchanging value.

As a result, what I learned is that when I wanted more money, I had to offer more value, and when I did, I didn't have to chase people down to sell them something; they found me and wanted to buy what I had.

And having clients that paid me month after month and year after year, was no longer a problem.

The question is, how does one actually go about offering more value?

Well, there is a mindset behind this idea of offering more value to get more money that I think I should explain.

Lesson 8: If You Want To Make More Money, Solve Bigger Problems.

For this lesson, there are two perspectives I want you to consider.

The first is that of a business owner, and the second is that of an employee who wants to make more money.

Let's say you run a business with about 50 employees.

You have a sales department, a tech department, an HR department, a fulfillment department, and assorted jobs from supervisors to managers and maintenance to secretaries.

Question. Is each of those jobs worth the same to your company?

It's an interesting question, isn't it?

Every position is necessary, but are they worth the same? How do you value what a position is worth and how much do you pay your employees in those positions?

If you've never thought of it, here is how it typically breaks down.

Executives are usually the highest-paid because they serve the most important function of keeping the business operating and profitable.

This is usually followed by the tech people. They're the ones that keep the infrastructure together so that businesses can operate in the first place.

Then there are salespeople. They bring in the money, and because of commission-based pay, they can sometimes out-earn tech people.

Then, there are the people in HR and accounting. They're the ones that are managing people and the money, including the taxes for the business.

Below them are the managers, secretaries, supervisors, and finally everyone else. All of these are support for the business. They handle the day-to-day functions that make the business operate.

Different companies have different structures, but in general, this is how everything is structured in a traditional company, where each position has a certain value to the company.

Higher-valued positions get more money, lower-valued ones get less because each solves a problem for your company.

When it comes to pay, most people think of time. Business owners think in terms of value. Not in terms of how much a person is worth, but how much a position is worth to the company.

As the business owner, you would have a budget and allocated spending for your departments, and the more important positions would have more money allocated to them.

Put another way, each position fulfills needs and solves problems, and the urgency of those needs and the size of the problems will usually dictate the money that gets allocated.

So, do you pay the mail clerk in shipping as much as the IT guy, or the secretary as much as the salesperson?

Remember, every job is important, but some positions have more value than others.

Do you pay the supervisor as much as an executive?

On the flip side of it, you are now the employee of that business.

You put in 40 hours a week, work your hardest, give them the best of your life during the day and come home on evenings simply exhausted, but you only make $10 per hour and it's barely enough to keep the lights on.

To really break even and maybe get a little bit ahead you need another $5 per hour.

How do you go about making more money from that business you work for?

Most people will continue to think about time and ask to work longer hours. Some will get a second job. A few, however, will look for a promotion.

Why a promotion? Have you ever wondered why promotions pay more money?

It's because, as a business owner, you'd put more money into jobs that meet more urgent needs and solve bigger problems for you, and as an employee, you'd look for a promotion to make more money because you that as you climb the position ladder, more money usually comes with it.

Here's what I'm saying.

The amount of money you earn is directly tied to the urgency of the needs you meet and the size of the problems you solve.

There's a reason why an attorney makes more money than a car mechanic. The mechanic solves small problems, and the attorney solves big ones.

This is why doctors make more money than store clerks. Anyone can check out your stuff at a counter and help you to your car, but not anyone can perform open-heart surgery and save your life.

Most people tend to believe that if they work hard they should be able to make as much money as they want, and while that ethically may be true, that's not how the world works, for anyone.

This is tied to the deservedness factor that people tend to have we talked about in chapter 3, but it's usually one-sided.

People equate how hard they work with how much they are owed, which is a problem because as you now know, that's not actually how money works.

Hard work is very important, but there's no real way to put a value how on hard someone works. If you don't believe that just ask any public-school teacher how hard they work and ask if they deserve more money.

So, you really can't put a price on hard work. This is why we have agreements and contracts.

When you accept a job or project, you're making an agreement with your employer or client, and it does not matter how hard or long you work because you are getting paid what both parties agreed to whether it's the amount per hour or the amount for the entire project.

It may not seem fair, but as you learned in chapter 3, what's fair is simply what two people have agreed to.

So, if you want to make more money on your job or charge more money for what you do, the best way is to solve bigger problems and meet more urgent needs.

Fixing small problems will get you paid small money and solving bigger problems will get you paid bigger money.

I want you to stop thinking like a consumer and start thinking like a business owner.

In the entrepreneurial world, the person who offers the most value makes the most money, even if it looks like they aren't doing anything different than anyone else.

The value isn't in how hard they work or how long they work. It's in what they're offering; the urgency of the needs they meet and the size of problems they solve.

If you want to make more money, solve bigger problems.

Lesson 9: Making Money Is A Skill Set.

In Chapter 2, I talked about the most important financial skill, *"The ability to make money from anywhere, at any time, no matter what the circumstances are."*

I called it a skill, but the truth is that it's a skill set, because many skills are needed to achieve that goal.

I had to learn about business, money, leadership, negotiation, sales, marketing, legal matters, taxes, business systems, and more, and each of those has several topics under them that are very important.

Then I had to put all of that knowledge together and apply what I was learning to start a business.

It sounds tedious, but the good news is that like any skill the more you do it the better you will become at it, and the more money you will be able to make because while it's hard to put a price on how hard someone works, putting a price on experience isn't very hard at all.

Just by learning these things you also increase your own value, which is something that will last a lifetime.

The other good news is that you don't have to learn every single skill at the same time, or even all of them before you can start making money.

You just have to learn a few basic things to start taking action. What you don't want to do is stay there on the beginner level. Once you get started, keep learning, keep applying, and keep growing.

Don't let that long list of things I had to learn overwhelm you.

The truth is that most of the work people have to do is mental so that they better understand how and why certain actions are taken first, before actually taking the actions.

As I'm sure you'll hear, if you haven't already, success is 90% mindset and 10% work. I'm not precisely sure if that is an exact percent or not, but it is true that the majority of your success will be in your head.

As far as introductions go, this book is taking care of much of the mindset work.

I've spent thousands of dollars and countless hours reading and studying and learning to even begin to write this. So, study this book well and remember all you can.

That being said, there are a few daily habits I would highly recommend focusing on first.

1. Don't let this be the only book on mindset you read. This book, while it has a lot of valuable information, is just the beginning of your education.

    My bookshelf is filled with books from business leaders and it keeps growing.

    Success happens every day, and there is a wealth of information to be learned from the examples and experiences of others.

    After all, if you don't learn from others' mistakes, you will have no choice but to learn from your own. Remember you want to avoid mistakes and one of the best ways is to learn what mistakes to avoid is by studying others.
2. Be clear in your goals so that the skills you develop will have a purpose. The last thing you want to do is learn something just for the sake of learning it, and it not being usable.

I wrote this book using information that I was able to apply to help me achieve my goals, and I began writing it as an exercise to help me solidify what I had learned.

I'd wager I could write two books with information that I found useless over the years. It was a huge waste of time and money.

This is going to sound weird, but you want to learn what you need to learn before you start learning it. In other words, find out first what you need to learn in order to do what you need to do, then learn it.

It's like a student figuring out what kind of degree they're going after. They find out ahead of time what classes they need to take, as well as prerequisites – what they should already know before taking the class.

Use the same approach with your business learning.

Don't do what I did and just jump right in without knowing the prerequisites or not having any idea of what you first need to learn.

There are a few books and videos I recommend specifically, and I have put together a list of resources that I found helpful, including a reading list, and a video playlist.

You'll find more information on that at the end of the book.

For right now though, it's time for the final lesson.

Lesson 10: Everything Is Sales.

Sales gets a bad rap, mostly because of movies and television, and the whole field has been branded in a relatively negative light because of the small percentage of sleazy salespeople who take advantage of people.

When I thought of sales, the image that came to my mind was the overweight car salesman in a cheap suit and bad, white loafers, smoking a cigar, telling me, *"this is the best deal on the planet!"*.

And a few years later, I really did have a sleazy car salesman in a cheap suit and bad loafers try to get me to buy an $8,000 used car for almost $20,000. When he said $495 per month for three years even his partner looked up at him like he was crazy.

So, you can probably imagine my initial disgust when I realized that I had to learn sales to be successful.

I'll be honest too. For a long time, I avoided it and looked for ways to make money without selling, only to realize something very important.

Everything is sales.

I should have known that too because the first big clue I got was having to buy something that promised to teach me how to make money without selling.

When the person who wanted to teach people how to make money without selling needed sales to get his course out there, it should have been a wake-up call for me to save my money and go learn sales.

I didn't do that though. I bought the course and kept trying to find ways to sell without actually selling.

I'll tell you now that it didn't work out, and when I finally did give and started learning sales, I fell in love with it because selling was not what I thought it was at all.

When I say everything is sales, I mean everything in our lives that requires the exchange of ideas. That is everywhere from the personal to the professional, and everything in between.

Here are a few examples.

Let's say you and your friends are planning an evening out and you're all wanting to do different things. If you want them to do what you want to do, then you have to convince them of your idea.

If they all accept your idea, then you just made a sale; you sold them on your idea.

When you apply for a job your resume is like an offer for a prospective hiring manager, and when you sit down for that interview, you're selling yourself as the best candidate for the job, out of many other people who you're competing against.

In relationships, the whole path from asking the other person out on a first date to marriage and kids is a lifelong sales process.

Guys know this very well.

First, you have to sell her on the idea that you're the guy she wants to make her boyfriend, so she picks you. Then after a while, you have to sell her on the fact that you're the guy she wants to spend the rest of her life with.

And when you're together, everything is a sale. Every decision that needs to be made, especially when there are disagreements, and you don't see eye-to-eye.

And when we mess up in a relationship, we have to sell our partners on the idea that they want to stay and not break up.

Learn sales. It will save your relationship! Haha.

I'm kidding obviously, but also kind of not, because how good you are at sales will affect your entire life.

Sales, as I now understand it, is simply the process of convincing someone to exchange something of value they have, for something of value you have.

It doesn't matter whether it's time, energy, resources, or money either, because "pay" can be anything.

As a real-life example, you ask the person out on a date, convince them that they're going to have a good time with you and if they say yes, you made a sale. You sold them having a good time with you and the pay you receive is their time and company.

You just have to make sure to deliver the goods or they will have buyer's remorse and you won't get a second date!

Another real-life example is when you go to a bank to open an account, you are the customer. The bank made an offer of security, money management, and assistance, you browsed their products, (account types), and then you purchased a product and give them your money.

(If you've never thought about how banks make money, do make a note to look that up).

Practically, for the next few days to a week, I want you to pay close attention to your conversations with people or pay attention to public conversations happening and see how many sales you can identify.

Sales are happening all the time and all around us, and more to the point, how good you are at sales will determine how much money you make, and as a result, the level of comfort you and your family will have, for your entire life.

The ability to convince or persuade others and get an exchange of value is super important, and it's one thing I wish I had learned in school.

Discussion.

When I've shared these with others, usually with clients that I consult for, the question of what the focus should be right now invariably arises.

The problem is that there was so much information given, taking the next step seems like an overwhelming task. It's information overload, especially if you're new, or relatively new to entrepreneurship. It's a lot to process.

That being said, if you're feeling overwhelmed, I encourage you to take a break; and I don't mean an hour or two. I mean take a few hours or even a day or so to let your mind process what you're learning.

I know it's bad advice for an author to tell their readers to stop reading, but I remember attending a high-impact business summit. It was three days of coaching, training, and mentoring, and that whole first day, my head hurt.

When you start learning to think differently, you are making physical changes to your brain. New neural pathways are being created, and as you begin to use them more, old pathways get overwritten.

So, take a break. Process. Let everything sink in, then come back and continue.

Chapter 5 – Bonus Lessons

Up until this moment, every chapter, and their subsequent lessons, even though there is no particular order, I did sort them in the order that I learned them, more or less, so each lesson seemed to build on the previous lessons.

There are, however, other lessons that I've learned that are just as important as the others to me but don't quite seem to fit into a progressive mold.

Bonus 1: Money Doesn't Change You. It Amplifies You.

You've probably heard it said that money changes people. You know, "somebody gets a lot of money and suddenly…" kinds of stories.

I'm not sure who started that, but it's not true.

Money doesn't change you. It affords you the opportunity to be who you truly are, much the same way that power does.

"You give someone a little bit of power and it goes right to their head," is the saying people use, but that's not true either.

People don't suddenly go bad.

The truth is that some people are only as good as they need to be in order to go through life with relative ease and comfort.

They need a job, and their friends and family, and help from time to time, and they can't afford to be bad or they'll find themselves out in the cold and in trouble.

It's a hard truth to learn, but there are covert and live covert lives.

The sweetest, kindest girl will quickly turn into a bridezilla once she gets that attention and power. They make shows about this now.

The most generous, loving guy will turn into a demanding, overbearing demon once they get that promotion and title.

The most supportive spouse will want a divorce when they win the lotto. There are actually "lottery pranks gone wrong" that prove this.

Now don't get me wrong. I'm not saying everyone is this extreme. These are just extreme, but real-life examples that I've experienced and have seen.

What I'm saying is that money doesn't change you. It just frees you to be who you already are.

You give a good person money, and they will do good things with it. You give a bad person money, and they will do bad things with it.

What kind of person are you? If money were no object, what kind of life would you lead?

Bonus 2: Don't Let Others Define What Success Looks Like For You.

It's one of the few downsides to this entrepreneur game I've found.

A lot of people try to define success according to what they think success looks like, and if you have a mentor, a lot of times people will model after their mentor's lifestyle and call that success.

It's very important that you set your own goals and define what success for you is because when you achieve it, it will keep you grounded.

For some, success is being able to party all the time. Fast cars, pretty girls, the hottest clubs.

For some, success is the freedom to travel wherever they want.

For some, success is giving their spouse the option to quit their job and be a full-time parent.

For some, success is getting out from under a mountain of debt and having an acre of land with their dream cottage on it.

For some, success is looking at their bank balance and seeing 2 commas.

For me, success was never having to commute to work ever again, and being able to work full time from home, and not having to wake up before the sun came up.

For you, success might be something completely different.

Whatever that looks like to you, make sure you're clear about that, because there are people who are quick to label others, and you do not want random people sucking the life out of your accomplishments.

Bonus 3: Don't Compare Yourself To Others.

This should be one of those "duh" advice moments, as important as it is to not let others define what success is for you, it is equally important that you don't define yourself by another person's success.

I used to do this.

I used to look at people who had achieved what I wanted to achieve, and I used to compare myself to them.

I used to ask myself, *"why am I not making any progress?"* and *"how are they getting results and I'm not?"* and many other questions.

It used to frustrate me because I worked extremely hard, and in my mind, I should be just as successful as whoever it was, I was comparing myself to.

I found out quickly that this was the fastest way to discourage myself and simultaneously slow my progress.

Understand too that while you are playing a game, you're not in a race against anyone else.

When you dive into the world of business and entrepreneurship, you will see and hear amazing stories of extraordinary people accomplishing great things and overcoming incredible obstacles.

You'll see people talking about and showing off spectacular results and winning awards for financial achievements.

They are not your competition.

They are people on their journeys, just as you are on your own, and they may be further ahead on their journey than you are on yours.

We all travel at our own speed and that's okay.

Do not compare yourself to others.

Bonus 4: Know What Game You're Playing.

This is one of those lessons that I recently learned, and it completely changed the way I do business, and it centers around game theory.

Remember I said that you are playing a game? You are playing the infinite game.

Let me explain.

In game theory, there is the infinite game, and there is the finite game.

In the finite game, there are known players, everyone agrees to rules, and there is an established objective that defines clear winners and losers.

Sports is a great example of a finite game.

In football, basketball, races, and many other sports, there are clearly defined rules like boundaries, zones, and penalties, and the game is over when someone has the highest score when the timer runs out, or they're the first to cross the finish line, they made the best time, etc.

The objective of the finite game is clear – beat your opponent and win the game.

And when the game is over, the game is over. Nobody says, *"let's go one more lap,"* or *"let's play another quarter"* because they think with one more round, they can come back.

The infinite game is basically the opposite.

There are known and unknown players, the rules aren't clearly defined, there are no clear objectives to win anything, and anyone can begin playing the game at any time.

The objective of the game is to keep the game going and continue playing until the other players run out of resources or simply drop out.

On top of that, anyone who has dropped out before can begin playing again.

The standard example of this is the Cold War. More than a dozen countries were involved in a non-violent war of ideologies opposed to Nazism, and there were two factions, (for and against).

As the war continued, when a country ran out of resources and was unable to continue playing, they simply dropped out.

It turns out, all the United States had to do to win was outspend everyone else, and eventually, everyone else dropped out.

When you pit an infinite player against an infinite player, the system is stable. When you pit a finite player against a finite player the system is stable.

The problem arises when you pit an infinite player against a finite player because the finite player is always trying to "be #1" or "beat the competition," while the infinite player is focused on continuing business.

In the long run, the finite player gets frustrated and drops out, because there are no clear objectives to base winning or losing on, and nobody has agreed to any rules.

They spend all of their resources on intangible and arbitrary objectives.

Meanwhile, the infinite player is focused on growing and serving customers and being in business and profitable for the next decade.

Know who the players in your market are. Study them, learn from them, always try to innovate, and get better, but understand that you are playing an infinite game.

You are your only competition.

You are not in business to beat everyone else. You are in business to serve others and continue being in business for as long as possible, whether it's 10 years, 50 years, 100 years, or more.

That is how you build legacies.

Business is an infinite game.

Bonus 5: Practice Empathy.

In business, empathy, the capacity to understand what a person is feeling from their point of view, is something I **strongly believe** is lacking today, and I believe that the path to true, lasting success involves empathy.

After all, how are you going to serve someone and not understand where they are coming from?

Here's a question.

Have you ever felt like you were being used for your money, or for how much you can perform, but never really valued for who you are as a person?

Whether it's at work and being under-appreciated, or at a restaurant or shopping and feel the only thing they value is your money?

It sucks, right? It's a horrible feeling.

Everyone wants to be appreciated. Everyone wants to feel like they matter, or that they have a voice and they're heard when they have a complaint or problem.

And in business, we tend to turn people into numbers; they're a payroll expense or a percent on an arbitrary performance chart.

I try not to do that and practice empathy for a few reasons, not the least of which is that it's the right thing to do.

First, it builds customer loyalty.

Back when I worked regular jobs, I was out doing collections and repo for furniture and appliances, and one of my customers gave me some advice that I'll never forget.

He said, *"A lot of people struggle these days with money and paying bills. Listen to this old man. Practice empathy and really get to know your customers. If you can do that, it doesn't matter what else they have going on, they will make sure and pay you, even before they pay anyone else. Treating people right goes a long way to building trust and loyalty"*.

I was always one to listen to my elders, so I practiced empathy, and discovered that he was right. While I worked there, I hardly ever had a problem with people not paying.

There were three or four other associates that had the same job as me, and at the end of every week when they were closing at 7% or 8% unpaid on their accounts, I was closing at 2% and 3% unpaid.

Later, when I became the assistant manager of the store and word got out, the business grew. More and more people become customers, and even old customers who had left, became customers again, all because I was the kind of person, they wanted to do business with.

They knew me. They liked me. They trusted me.

I made practicing empathy a way of life and I've found that the rewards go beyond the personal and they stretch into business.

When I understand my customers and really know them, I use that knowledge to create better products and services. I serve them better, which is the whole point of business.

Plus, because my customers know, like, and trust me, I get a lot of referrals. In fact, more than half of my customers are repeat or referral customers from other customers.

I don't have to spend a lot of money on advertising as a result. Practicing empathy is something that I think every business should do.

I'm not saying be a pushover or cave into unreasonableness. Just take a few extra steps to ask questions, listen to them, and understand what they're going through and where they're coming from.

Customers are not numbers. They are people.

Discussion.

I hope you enjoyed this little bonus chapter and were able to learn something valuable from it, even if it was mostly personal to me.

And hopefully, if you took a break as suggested at the end of chapter 4, you've had time to process what you're learning and really let some of the lessons sink in.

I stay that because the very next step for you is the action-taking part and I don't want you to operate from a position of being overwhelmed.

So, take a break if you need to, and when you're ready, I'll see you in the next chapter.

Chapter 6 – Method & Mechanism

This entire book so far has been centered around money mindsets, and even though there were some references to method and mechanism, we haven't really covered them, so we are going to do that now.

In truth, there are many methods and many mechanisms that make money and the same two, common word covers them all. They are business and system.

Whenever someone says, *"I'm building a business,"* or *"I have a system to make money,"* they're all referring to the same thing – infrastructure.

Before I get too far ahead, let me explain my point of view a bit, maybe define a few terms so that you understand where I'm coming from.

I was trained as a civil engineer before I decided I wanted to do what I'm doing now. I studied physics, chemistry, architecture, land surveys, road systems, geography, and science.

I have a very analytical and structured approach to understanding and breaking down things in simple step-by-step instructions for others to follow. I can read and create blueprints, and I think like a blueprint.

I had a lot of trouble adjusting to thinking like an entrepreneur because there are a lot of abstract points of views and that doesn't work well for engineers.

We understand abstract just fine, but abstract doesn't work when you're trying to build something. You need a plan. You need a blueprint.

And in the business world, there are many.

So, what I did was break all of them down from being something abstract to something actual because I needed to share this, and I needed to do it in a way that makes sense and for it to be something that's duplicable and applicable.

Now, let's define a few terms.

Infrastructure is the physical and organizational structure of something – a building, a road, a business, and so on. It is how something is put together, and organized, and how it operates as a whole.

Inside of an infrastructure, there are methods and mechanisms.

Methods are the procedures for accomplishing or approaching something. When someone asks, *"how does it work?"* this is what they're after.

Mechanisms are the actual parts that make everything work.

Methods and mechanisms together make up a system, which aptly defined as a set of things working together, to include procedure, (methods), and parts (mechanisms).

And now that you understand those three things, you can break down almost anything and understand it.

If you look at a car, you're seeing the infrastructure, and inside it, you're going to have parts and how they work individually, and you'll be able to understand how they all work together as a system.

If you can diagram it out, you have a blueprint, and you can build a car of your own.

You can do the same for just about anything from a simple pen to a washing machine, to a house, to a skyscraper… to business.

Now that you're armed with an analytical mind, let's break down business itself.

In order to make money in any business, whether you operate online or offline, or whether you're working in a brick-and-mortar building, or chilling on your bed with a laptop, (like I'm doing), you must have an infrastructure with systems in place, (methods and mechanisms).

I've analyzed countless dozens of businesses and all of the successful businesses have the same infrastructure.

Like cars, successful businesses come in different shapes and sizes, and they have different purposes and do different things, but when you break them down, they're all the same.

You must, at the very least, have these 5 things in common.

1. A product or service to offer. It doesn't matter if it's your product, or someone else's product, or a service of some kind; it can be offline, online, or a combination of both. This can be physical, (i.e., books, stationery, household goods, electronics, etc.), or digital products, (audio files, eBooks, video, blog posts, etc.).
2. A system in place that allows you to accept payments and deliver products and services to customers once they are purchased.
3. A method to connect, collect and follow up with leads and customers. A lead is when someone gives you their information in exchange for information about your business or offer. This is typically a name, email address, and phone number.
4. A system to acquire traffic. You need marketing to go out to get people to come to your store, your website, your place of business. It can be free traffic or paid traffic.
5. A system to support customers, so that people who buy from you can have questions answered and have problems addressed.

I know that for some, it might sound like a lot to have in place, but it doesn't have to be.

Once upon a time, when starting a business meant getting thousands and thousands of dollars in funding, getting a physical building, and hiring staff to even get off the ground, maybe, but we don't live in that time anymore.

We live in the amazing age of the Internet, where you don't have to be a pioneer like Steve Jobs and build a dream team out of your garage to create something and build from the ground up.

And you don't have to be gifted like many of the other giants of industry we know today.

They had to do it the hard way. You don't, and many of the things you need today are either free or very affordable.

So, what I'm going to do is break down one of my businesses into its parts so that you can actually see and understand how this works in real life.

It's a very simple 3-plus income stream model that I use as a basis for all of my businesses.

I used this first to make money when I was broke, then I used it to make money to start my business and to pay for marketing, and now I use this as a way to establish myself in a market or industry and attract customers.

My 3-Plus Income Stream Blueprint Overview.

I'm calling this a blueprint overview because the goal isn't to go completely through the process. The goal is that you will be able to understand the process from a real-world perspective, and possibly duplicate this and do it on your own.

So, let's walk through my set-up process from start to finish and step-by-step.

Step 1: Find something to sell.
There are actually a few approaches to this, and I'll talk about them, but before you just run out to find something to sell, there is a mindset to consider.

As a general rule of thumb, I tend to stick to what I already know when looking for products or services to sell.

What I mean is that we all have interests, hobbies, skills, knowledge, and experience, even work experience, that makes us a bit of experts in our own way.

What are you good at? What do you have experience in? What can you teach someone? What have problems have you overcome in your life? Do people come to you for advice, and if so, about what?

All of these questions and more are valuable; what you know is valuable.

Understanding this, when I look for a product, I tend to stick within the boundaries of what I know. The downside is that most people only know what they've been exposed to and/or have studied or had experience in.

The upside is that now you have a reason to discover, learn, and grow.

In reality, there are only two ways to find products and services to sell.

1. You offer someone else's products and services, like affiliate offers.
2. You create your own products and services.

When you decide what route you're going to go, the rest is up to your imagination.

For affiliate products, I usually start with what I know, and I tend to look for products or services that I would use myself, or would recommend to others, centered around what problems people face.

Does it solve the problem(s) or make the problem easier? If the answer is "yes" then it becomes a good candidate.

When I decide to create my own products and services, there are a lot more options open to me.

For example, I can look at my past, identify problems I've overcome and how I overcame them, and create a product that teaches that.

Or, using my knowledge and work experience, I can look for problems in my field that other people have, and I create guides that offer tips, tricks, and hacks that people could use to be better at their jobs.

I can broker services.

What that means is that I can look for a problem someone has, find someone with a solution to that problem, and put them together, and take a cut for myself.

I can leverage my skills as a programmer to create online software for people to use.

Note: Regarding leveraging my skills, everyone has something they can do related to their profession that they can also leverage to make money in other ways.

I can teach people what I know through books, audio, video, and even in person, and I can inform.

There are many ways to create products and services, but the ones I mentioned are the ways that I actually do.

In the blueprint, I choose the last one mentioned, to inform.

I find a topic that people are trying to learn, something that I already have experience in and know, and start creating digital content that people want to read.

Content varies from articles I write to videos I create, to audio files I record, and more.

What I'm selling is information.

Step 2: Build the infrastructure.
Once you know what you're going to sell, you can take care of the next three items on the list with one thing – a simple blog.

Let's break the setup down into steps.

   a. First, register a domain name, (something relevant to the topic your information is about), get some cheap hosting, and install blog software, (I prefer WordPress).
   b. Second, you're going to get a merchant account like PayPal or Stripe. This will allow you to accept donations and create buy now and subscribe buttons to put on your blog.
   c. Third, on your new hosting account, you're going to create an email address for support. I like to use hello@<your domain>, help@<your domain>, support@<your domain>, or something along those lines.

      That email address will be included in any purchase customers make so if they have a problem or a question, they can email you.
   d. Fourth, you're going to set up your blog with plugins that will allow you to place ads on your site. I prefer using Advanced Ads.

      Just follow the instructions. They are simple and they have plenty of help docs available if you're stuck.

      What's important is that while you're setting it up, you turn on the settings for Google AdSense™, then sign up for it.

      This is the first stream of income.
   e. Fifth, you're doing to install another plugin that allows you to syndicate content from other creators using feeds. I syndicate content from others for a couple of reasons.

      First, I do it to create massive amounts of content. The way that blogging works, the more you post, the more traffic you get, so I leverage that. On top of that, it makes great filler content and takes the pressure off of you from having to constantly create new content all the time.

      And second, I syndicate for branding. Remember that you're selling information, so if you're known as a source of information, people will seek you out.

My preferred plugin is called CyberSEO Lite (CyberSyn). It is also very simple and has a lot of support.

This is very important – before you go out there and start syndicating content from popular places, **get permission**!

If you don't get permission to syndicate other people's content, you can get sued, so get permission and get it in writing. Protect yourself.

f. Sixth, and this is the hard part; you're going to create all of the content that you're going to sell.

Once I know what I want to share, I research everything about it and create a kind of syllabus or outline, then create that content and have it ready to go.

This is by far the hardest part of all of it because as a personal goal, I try to have 52 articles about my subject already written and ready to go, (one article per week).

That way, all I have to do is write them and schedule them in WordPress and they're automatically published every week.

You don't have to do all 52 in one go though. If you're a busy person, you can post one article a week, or you can write a few articles at a time, publish one, and schedule the others.

That way, you're always posting future content and you're not always trying to catch up because you missed a week.

g. Seventh, with personal content creation and one stream of income out of the way, I begin finding affiliate products I can sell.

This is my second stream of income.

Again, sticking with what I know, and staying with products relevant to my content, I'll place ads for affiliate products on my site blog, and I will also buy a product, try it out, and write a review.

At the end of the review, I'll place a link to it and ask customers to buy it if they feel they can benefit from it.

h. Eighth is the third stream of income, creating my own product to sell. This can quickly become two or more income streams by itself.

   What I do is start looking for problems I can solve using the content I'm already publishing.

   I find these largely through web searches and online forums. A great place to find out what problems people have is to check out companies in the market that you publish and check out their bad reviews.

   If they're part of the Better Business Bureau, you can look up their company online and see if they have any negative ratings.

   Another way I find out what people need is to just ask them.

   On some of those forums, or on social media sites, I'll create an account and just ask people if they need help with anything, or if they have any questions.

   Sometimes what I'll do is look at the reviews of affiliate products I sell, make a note of what people are not happy about, and I'll find a solution, then make that a product that I will sell alongside the affiliate offer.

   The products I usually create are guides and eBooks people can purchase and download, (this book is one of them).

   In general, I sell them the exact same way I sell affiliate products, with a few exceptions.

   I don't just let people download my products just like that.

   I create a squeeze page, which is simply a landing page that tells the user what they're going to get/learn/solve their problem/etc. if they enter their name and email address into the form. In other words, they become a lead.

   Once they've opted in, I give them the information to solve their problem, (that's what they are there for), and at the end, depending on whether they were introduced to a solution, would need help implementing the solution, or want to hire me to do it, I'd ask them to buy, donate, or hire me.

   That is over-simplified and there is a lot more that goes into that whole process, but I wanted you to understand how it's done.

If you want to learn more about this process, I will have resources for you at the end of the book.

i. Ninth, with everything in place, all that's left for you to do is optimize your blog with proper SEO. Don't worry, this is simple enough to do with a plugin.

There are a few plugins that make the process easy. The two most popular are AllInOneSEO and Yoast SEO.

I actually don't use either of them.

I use a plugin called Squirrly. It has a guided setup that will let you walk you through what you need to know with SEO, and it provides a lot of tooltips, as well as having a guide on every post so that you can optimize each post you make.

j. Once everything is set up and ready to go, all you have to do is begin marketing and promoting to start driving traffic.

This includes activities like:

 - Using a service like Ping-o-matic to "ping your blog posts" so they get syndicated across the internet.
 - Sharing content on social media and starting discussions.
 - Going back to the forums where people were asking questions and sharing the solutions, and asking people to message you if they want to know more.
 - Submitting your domain name to search engines like Google, Bing, and Yahoo!.
 - Offer guest posts, where you publish content for others and let them promote their own articles on your site. That's free traffic.
 - Buying advertising from trusted sources.
 - Running paid ads.
 - And more.

When it comes to driving traffic there are literally dozens of ways to do it, and some are unique to blogging, which is one of the reasons why I use blogging.

Plus, the longer you blog, the more and more traffic you get organically if it's active.

There are other things you can do as well with that infrastructure set up, like run an ad program yourself where other businesses pay you to run their ads.

You can also have sponsored posts, where others who want to be found on your site pay you to publish their articles for them.

You can install a membership plugin and start a monthly paid support service where people pay you a little bit every month to provide some sort of consulting and/or support.

Or one of my favorites, as you build a bigger and bigger list from selling your own products, others can pay you to place ads in your emails to your customers.

Discussion.

I know this section might sound a little bit complicated, but I promise you it's not. It might actually have taken me longer to write this chapter than it does to set this up.

With exception to creating the content you need; you can have this entire thing set up in less than a day, even if you're new and have no idea what you're doing.

The technology is already built for you and it's mostly plug-and-play.

The first time you do it all the way through, you'll realize just how easy it is, and as you get better and better at operating the business, you'll find that you can scale and turn three income streams into four, five, six and more.

And this brings us full circle back to where this book started – mindset.

Making money is a skill, and the more you do it, the better you will become at it, and the more money you will make.

And the best way to get started is to just get started and start building experience.

Before you run out and reserve domain names and such though, I would highly suggest that you start with coming up with an idea first on paper.

Do the research, follow the instructions, and create your own blueprint, and use free blog services to test with.

Learn and become familiar with the process, and after you're ready, then start building for real.

If you would like some help with this process, you'll find out how to get help in the last chapter, **Resources and Recommended Learning**.

Chapter 7 – Resources and Recommended Learning

Before we get into the resources and recommended learning, congratulations on getting this far in the book!

I won't lie. This book is not an easy read, especially if you're new to the entrepreneur industry.

I've learned a lot over the past 8 years in business and these are just *some* of the things that I've learned, and I've tried to explain them as best I am currently able.

There is a lot of information here and I am happy to share it.

The being said, there are some practical things I would highly recommend.

1. Learn about how money works. Now that you plan to start making money outside of a traditional job structure, there is a lot to learn about finance, and the higher your financial IQ becomes, the better off you'll be.
2. Learn sales. Learn the process of making offers, overcoming objections, and closing sales. This will serve you in more ways than I can possibly count.
3. Become a student of marketing. Learn how to drive traffic and get leads. This is the lifeblood of every company. You can have the greatest product in the world, but if nobody knows about it, it's not doing you any good; and there are dozens of strategies that you can choose from.
4. Study leadership and learn about influence and persuasion. Being able to build a following of people is a powerful skill to have and it can make your path to success go much faster.
5. Find a mentor and take business training. I don't mean to sign up at a local college to study business administration either. I mean find someone who is an entrepreneur, who is successful, and has accomplished what you want to accomplish yourself and model after them. Learn from them, buy their training, go to their events.

To aid you with this, I've created a free membership that includes:

- Recommended reading lists about leadership, finance and money management, sales, marketing strategies, and more.
- Video training about mindset and business.
- Business training via courses and masterminds.
- Discounts on services to help you start and operate your business.
- And many more resources, including more details and resources to help you implement the 3-plus income stream blueprint for yourself.

To get access, please visit https://dexternelson.net/members/ to register for free.

Notes

I've made sure to include a couple of blank pages for you to jot down thoughts and ideas. It's better than writing on a napkin!

Money Mindset, Method & Mechanism

An Entrepreneur's Journey from Trapped on A Job to Freedom Working from Home

... and the Most Important Things I Ever Learned About Business and Money.

By Dexter Nelson

www.ingramcontent.com/pod-product-compliance
Lightning Source LLC
Chambersburg PA
CBHW081454220526
45466CB00008B/2640